Small Steps to Bigger Love

Small Steps to Bigger Love

A PRACTICAL GUIDE TO MARRIAGE
AS A SPIRITUAL PRACTICE

DEBBY GULLERY

Copyright © 2015 by Debby Gullery
Second Edition © 2022

debbygullery.com
Contact Debby: coachgullery@gmail.com

All rights reserved. No part of this publication may be reproduced, stored in a retrieval system or transmitted, in any form, or by any means, electronic, mechanical, recorded, photocopied, or otherwise, without the prior written permission of both the copyright owner and the above publisher of this book, except by a reviewer who may quote brief passages in a review.

The scanning, uploading, and distribution of this book via the internet or via any other means without the permission of the publisher is illegal and punishable by law. Please purchase only authorized electronic editions and do not participate in or encourage electronic piracy of copyrightable materials. Your support of the author's rights is appreciated.

Print: 978-0-578-35144-5

Printed in the United States of America

Contents

	Introduction 11	
1	Marriage as a Spiritual Practice 13	
2	Whole Mates or Soul Mates? 17	
3	Oh, The Questions We Ask! 20	
4	How to Change Your Partner 22	
5	Notice and Appreciate the Good Things 25	
6	The Problem with Problems 27	
7	Commitment Counts and Maintenance Matters . . 31	
8	Generous Listening 35	
9	Talking Points 39	
10	A Crash Course in Safety 42	
11	Reducing Toxic Tendencies 47	
12	Talking About Hot Topics Without Burning Up! . . 51	
13	What Were You Expecting? 55	
14	Fostering Friendship 60	
15	Are We Having Fun Yet? 63	
16	Marriage is Always an Inside Job 67	
17	Staying Open To Forgiveness 73	
18	Boundaries and Why We Need Them 77	
19	Learn Your Partner's Love Language 82	

20	When Planets Collide........................86
21	Core Beliefs and Spirituality 91
22	The Marriage Bed............................95
23	Goals, Growth and Guts.....................100
24	Editing Your Script..........................103
25	Tending to Your Spending...................106
26	A Word on the In-laws......................111
27	Recalibrating After A Life-Changing Event......115
28	Blended Families............................118
29	Seasons of Love 122
29	Becoming a Blessing to Each Other 126
30	Small Steps to Bigger Love 128
	Small Group Study Guide....................131
	About the Author 146

Dedicated to my husband Jonathan, who helped me become the person I am today, and taught me more about love and loyalty than anyone else on the planet. And to our three children, who have grown into kind and loving adults and whose company I greatly enjoy.

The Love Book

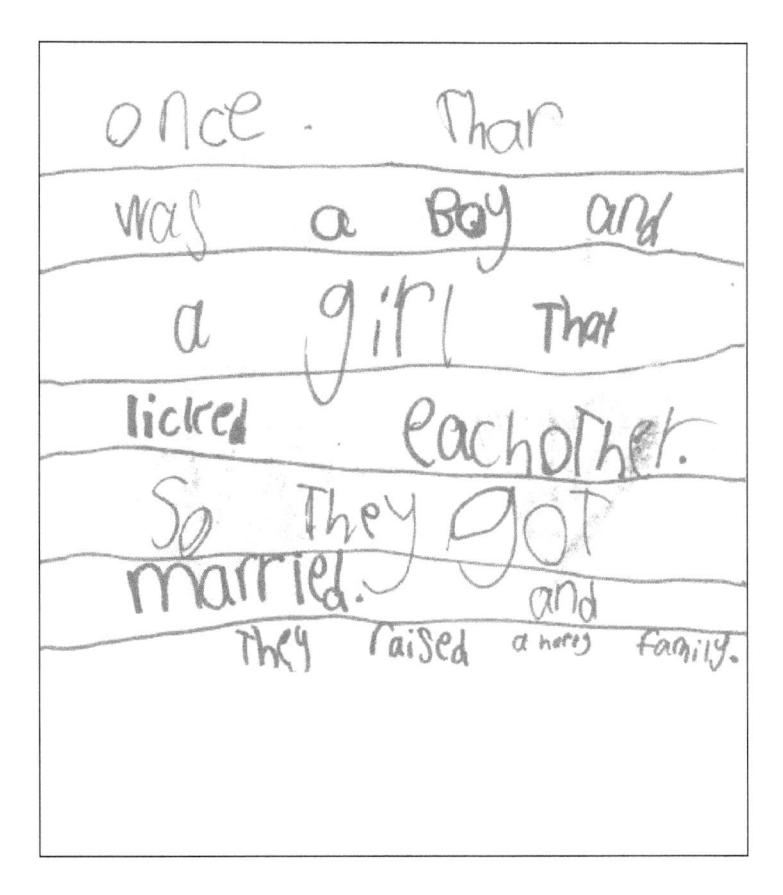

once. Thar was a Boy and a girl That licked eachother. So They got married. and They raised a happy family.

Given to me by a 2nd grade student at indoor recess, Brookside School, Ossining, New York

To marry is the biggest risk in human relations that a person can take... If we commit ourselves to one person for life this is not, as many people think, a rejection of freedom; rather it demands the courage to move into all the risks of freedom, and the risk of love which is permanent; into that love which is not possession, but participation.

—Madeleine L'Engle

Marriage is the greatest test in the world...but now I welcome the test instead of dreading it. It is much more than a test of the sweetness of temper, as people sometimes think; it is a test of the whole character and affects every action.

—T.S. Eliot

Introduction

Drawing on my own marriage and my work as a marriage educator and relationship coach, I have discovered that marriage is fertile ground for spiritual and emotional growth.

So much so, that I will venture to say that marriage might be designed to help us grow. If you are married or in a long-term committed relationship, you may have already experienced this to be true.

Being married naturally offers us endless opportunities to stretch our capacity to love and to practice living from our core beliefs. Our marriages have the uncanny ability to reveal exactly what we need to work on. Luckily, our love and commitment towards each other also motivates us to want to change.

Why is that? It is because within our marriages, the stakes are the highest and the rewards are the greatest!

I invite you to consider that investing in your marriage has the potential to be your best and most effective spiritual practice.

To help you in this sacred endeavor, I offer this book as a step-by-step guide in the journey of a lifetime!

1

Marriage as a Spiritual Practice

Anything worth doing requires practice and having a good marriage does too. One can practice choosing happiness over the need to be right or to always win the argument. One can practice playfulness, generosity, and openness. One can practice having both a strong voice and a gentle touch. One can practice calming things down and warming them up even when the other person is behaving badly. One can practice taking a firm position on things that matter—a position that is not negotiable under relationship pressures.

It helps to know the rules, which you might prefer to think of as pretty good ideas to consider.... Small, positive changes have a way of morphing into more generous, expansive ones. Your relationship thanks you in advance.

—Harriet Lerner, PhD.

In the last 50 years society has gone through many rapid and substantial changes. Some of these changes have impacted the expectations we now have for our marriages and intimate relationships. I think it's safe to say that we expect more from our marriages than we ever have before. We want our partners to be our best friends and the best of lovers, and some of us hope that our partnerships will also reflect our common core values.

In addition to those desires, many people are striving to live more meaningful and authentic lives and are recognizing that their most important relationships can be helpful in achieving that. Why is that?

Navigating our significant relationships helps us to develop compassion and loving kindness. It makes sense that in the relationships that matter the most to us, where love, trust and loyalty are central, endless opportunities for growth would naturally occur.

But personal growth can be perplexing and tricky. We all like to see ourselves as loving people, who care about the environment, and the future of the planet. We can convince ourselves of our spirituality because we meditate or pray regularly, or volunteer at the food bank. But I would like to suggest that in most cases, the real measure of our growth as human beings is most evident in the way we function in our important relationships.

Realistically, it can often seem easier to love the world than to love our partners, especially when they are not living up to our expectations. Or when we are confronted by a partner who has expectations and needs that require our investment and effort to meet.

Our true character is revealed in the hundreds of choices we make every day; whether it is to follow our conscience or not, to prefer the needs of another or not, or to give when we just do not feel like it.

In this way, our spouses act as mirrors for us by reflecting to us the best and the worst in ourselves. When we are married, we have opportunities to see how good we are at loving and respecting each other many times a day.

When we notice, appreciate, and embrace these opportunities, our marriages naturally become instrumental to our emotional and spiritual growth. In other words, the way we look at our relationships determines what we get out of them.

For example, what would it be like if we saw our most important relationships as the actual path to our wholeness? What would happen if we saw marriage as transformative spiritual practices?

I think we might treat our partners and families very differently. If we were to look at our relationships as central to our spiritual growth, we would be forced to pay attention to our actions and attitudes more often. Paying attention, being mindful and living in the moment, are all decidedly spiritual things to do.

In this way, challenges shift from being scary and undesirable to opportunities for growth, and our marriages become center stage.

So how does this really work? Well, first we need to become more intentional about our internal growth in general. And then we need to start paying attention to ourselves—to our attitudes, our thoughts, our words, and our actions. We need to expect growth and look for it. Personal growth does not happen automatically—we have to work at it.

For example, we can choose to do things that move us in the direction of connection and love. We can begin to treat our relationships as laboratories for our daily spiritual practice, that can help us to move closer towards becoming the authentic, loving people we want to be.

The people we love and live with every day naturally become the ones to point out any bad habits or selfishness we might need to work on, but they are also the ones who keep us motivated to continually invest and improve ourselves.

A good marriage requires commitment to constant personal growth and change. It also requires huge amounts of honesty and courage. These are the necessary ingredients to build marriages that have our core values at their center. And when we approach our relationships in this way, we become true spiritual partners.

As spiritual partners, we choose to look out for each other's well-being and search for ways to enrich and enhance each other. This requires daily investment of time and energy.

Take a moment to look at your spouse and thank them for their commitment to you and your relationship. And then take some time to talk together about how your relationship can become more of an integral part of your growth and development.

SPIRITUAL PRACTICE

1. Ask yourself how you can intentionally invest in your marriage today?
2. Think about how you could act in a loving way towards your partner today?
3. With your partner, reflect on the ways you have helped each other to grow in positive ways.

2

Whole Mates or Soul Mates?

People think a soul mate is your perfect fit, and that's what everyone wants. But a true soul mate is a mirror, the person who shows you everything that is holding you back, the person who brings you to your own attention so you can change your life.
—Elizabeth Gilbert, "Eat, Pray, Love"

To say that one waits a lifetime for his soulmate to come around is a paradox. People eventually get sick of waiting, take a chance on someone, and by the art of commitment become soulmates, which takes a lifetime to perfect.
—Criss Jami, "Venus in Arms"

The term 'soul mate' means different things to different people, but in general, I think it tends to give us unrealistic expectations about love. Often, we assume that if someone is our soulmate than the relationship will be easy.

The extension of that idea can lead people to think that if things are not going well or if they are too hard, it must be because their partner is not really their soul mate.

On an unconscious level, believing in and searching for our soulmate can simply reflect our deep desire to be loved by someone unconditionally, rather than a more mature approach to love that offers mutual support and love.

It conjures up magical thinking, luck, and very little responsibility. It allows people to think that there is only one person in the whole universe that can be their soul mate—it gets people looking and praying for something outside of themselves, instead of investing in the person who is right in front of them.

For these reasons, I coined the term "whole mates". What is the difference between soul mates and whole mates? A whole mate is someone we become over time. A whole mate is a work in progress. Whole mates co-create each other through intentional spiritual practice.

The real work in creating spiritual partnerships is not in finding the right person, but in *becoming* the right person, someone who is *capable* and *willing* to build such a partnership. And then it is about what happens *after* we have committed to each other.

A whole mate is not necessarily someone who will always be fun to be with or make us feel good. A whole mate is so much more than that. It is someone who helps us discover what is deep in our souls, even if what is there is hard to embrace.

A whole mate always has our best interest at heart and stays by us through thick and thin. We become whole mates for each other with time, investment, and commitment. There is nothing better.

> *"Real isn't how you are made," said the Skin Horse. "It's a thing that happens to you. When a child loves you for a long, long time, not just to play with, but REALLY loves you, then you become Real."*
> *"Does it hurt?" asked the Rabbit.*
> *"Sometimes," said the Skin Horse, for he was always*

truthful. "When you are Real you don't mind being hurt."

"Does it happen all at once, like being wound up," he asked, "or bit by bit?"

"It doesn't happen all at once," said the Skin Horse. "You become. It takes a long time. Generally, by the time you are Real, most of your hair has been loved off, and your eyes drop out and you get loose in the joints and very shabby. But these things don't matter at all, because once you are Real you can't be ugly, except to people who don't understand."

—Margery Williams, *The Velveteen Rabbit*

SPIRITUAL PRACTICE

Take some time individually to make a list of qualities and attitudes that you feel are important in a whole-mate partnership and then share that list with each other. Notice which things both of you have written down and make a goal to strengthen one of those areas in your relationship.

3

Oh, The Questions We Ask!

At the end of the day, the questions we ask of ourselves determine the type of people that we will become.
—Leo Babauta

As we work toward looking at our marriages as our spiritual practice, we may also have to alter the way we think. A good way to begin the shift is to start noticing the things we tell ourselves and the questions we ask ourselves. Our questions reveal a great deal about the way we are thinking.

For example, when we get angry at our partners for something, many of us tend to ask ourselves, "Why are they doing this to me?" This may not be the best question to ask at that moment because it assumes two things that may or may not be true.

The first is that our partner is doing what they are doing *on purpose* to upset us. And if we assume this, it is hard to have a good attitude towards them.

The second assumption is that they are *aware* of how much they are upsetting us, and this is rarely the case. We know, from our own experiences, that we are often unaware of how our words and actions are impacting others.

Instead of asking that question when our partner upsets us, what would happen if instead, we asked ourselves one of the following:

- What can I learn about myself and the way I am reacting to this?
- Why am I having such strong feelings about what my partner is doing?

Asking either of these questions puts the responsibility where it really belongs—with us—and helps us to learn more about ourselves.

If we are trying to become the best people we can be and trying to help our partners accomplish the same thing, then we need to ask ourselves different, and smarter, questions.

Here is one more excellent question to ask ourselves when we are upset with our beloved: If I am being true to my core beliefs, how should I react in this moment?

Asking ourselves these questions can literally alter the trajectory of our spiritual and emotional growth. They can help us to shift our attitude from one of blaming to one of taking responsibility. When we make asking these questions of ourselves habitual, we can change both our perspective and our loving relationships.

SPIRITUAL PRACTICE

Make a goal to practice asking the following questions of yourselves whenever you feel annoyed, disappointed, or angry with your partner. Try it for a week and then discuss what it was like for both of you.

- What can I learn about myself and the way I am reacting to this?
- Why am I having such strong feelings about what my partner is doing?
- If I am being true to my core values, how should react in this moment?

4

How to Change Your Partner

It's been said that most of us plan more for a Christmas party than we do for our lives. And when it comes to achieving wholeness, to building a solid sense of identity and self-worth, we want something to happen to us. Like magic, we want to be zapped with an insight, with wisdom, or even a mystical experience that will change us. The problem is you don't catch a sense of self-worth from reading a book or attending a seminar or seeing a therapist. Self-worth comes from hard work. It is earned. It comes from dreaming to make a difference and then making the sacrifices to make your dreams a reality. Wholeness is forged from your efforts. You will never achieve it as a passenger; you must sit in the driver's seat.
—Drs. Les and Leslie Parrott, "Relationships"

Let's start with how to change our partners—oops! We can't! Get that out of the way right now. That is his or her job. Here's a secret: The only way to get someone to change is to love and accept them to the best of your ability. Then they will *want* to become the best they can be and will have the confidence and support they need to do so. It is the "Catch 22" of loving.

Couples who are successful and doing well are *not* that

way because they were lucky enough to come from stable, loving homes, and it's *not* just because they have excellent communication skills. It is also not because they found an especially wonderful person to marry. What gives them an edge are *their attitudes* towards each other and their relationship.

Happy couples practice an overall feeling of generosity towards each other and make effort to develop the attitude of '*I am on your side*' or '*I have your back*'. They focus on building good habits, they work at keeping their difficulties in perspective, and they try hard to be nice to each other even when they are angry or stressed. They give each other the benefit of the doubt and they *assume the best in each other.*

Cultivating this kind of attitude towards each other is one of the kindest things that we can do for ourselves too. It puts us in control, and it allows us to experience the pleasure of giving to someone we love. Both things are empowering.

This does not mean that we do everything for our partners or excuse them of all their shortcomings and mistakes. It is not about giving in or losing control, and it does not mean that we do the internal work *for* them that they need to do for themselves. It just means that we *choose* to be kind, and we *choose* to focus on their strengths and their goodness.

By the way, this can be especially hard to do when they are driving us crazy and we are tempted to react in unspiritual ways!

Here is a trick that can be helpful in those moments: Imagine your partner is hanging from the edge of a cliff by their fingernails. I suggest this because when people are acting in ways that are upsetting to us, it is usually because they are struggling themselves, and are temporarily incapable of disciplining their behavior. This way of looking at our partners encourages compassion rather than anger and disappointment.

If we work on improving ourselves, our efforts will naturally spill over and affect our partners and our relationships. Imagine what might happen if we made effort to find something to be grateful for about our partner each day. How might that affect them?

What if we noticed and complimented the positive traits we see in our partners on a regular basis? Might that make a difference to them or to our relationship? Of course!

So, let us strive to see the best in our partners and to behave with kindness and generosity towards them as often as we can. This is the real key to getting our partners to change.

SPIRITUAL PRACTICE

Make a goal to find something to be grateful for in your partner. Do this every day for one week. Write these down and at the end share your list with each other.

MARRIAGE MANTRAS

1. I will assume the best in my partner today.
2. I will practice generosity and kindness with them today.
3. I will work on expanding my capacity to love instead of trying to change them.

5

Notice and Appreciate the Good Things

What you focus on grows, what you think about expands, and what you dwell upon determines your destiny.

—Robin Sharma

Isn't it always easier for us to notice what *is not* going well or what our partners are doing to *annoy* us, rather than what they are doing to support us? It takes real effort to begin noticing the good stuff and the good things our partners are doing.

But that is just the first step. Once we notice these things, then we must *acknowledge* them. We need to say thank you sometimes and remember to express our appreciation.

In her seminal article, 'What Shamu Taught Me About a Happy Marriage', Amy Sutherland reveals what she learned about marriage while investigating the training of whales. She reports that the central lesson she learned was the importance of rewarding behavior she liked and ignoring behavior she did not. As she puts it, "You don't get a sea lion to balance a ball on the end of its nose by nagging."

In her article, she also describes how she used this new information to improve her relationship with her husband. She says she began thanking him for every little thing he did that she appreciated, and purposely ignored everything that bothered her.

She realized through this experiment that the most essential ingredient for domestic bliss was for her to change her own behavior.

What we focus on is what grows, so we want to focus on what is good in each other and strengthen that. Appreciation is powerful stuff. Let us practice it with our partners.

SPIRITUAL PRACTICE

Notice something good that your partner did or said today and *comment* on it. Try to do this at least once a day for a week. Note what changes, if anything, in the way you feel and in the way your partner responds to you. *Practice appreciation.*

Valuing One Another Exercise

In the spaces below, finish the following sentences and share your answers with each other.

- What I admire most about you is…
- One of my favorite memories is….
- I am glad you are _____ and I am not.
- One of the funniest things you have ever done is…
- One of my proudest memories of you is…
- I like it when you…
- One thing you do in our marriage to help it grow is…

Adapted from *The Eight Habits of a Successful Marriage*, by Stephen Covey

6

The Problem with Problems

When it rains, it pours. Maybe the art of life is to convert rough times to great experiences: We can choose to hate the rain or dance in it.
—Joan Marques

Every problem is a gift—without problems we would not grow.
—Anthony Robbins

Life is full of problems, big and small; therefore, negotiating and solving problems is a huge part of marriage and it *matters* how well we do it! So how can we have a more spiritual and effective approach to problem-solving?

First, it is interesting to note that research suggests that close to 80% of the problems couples struggle with do not need to be solved at all!

It seems that what really matters is for each person to feel that their partner genuinely understands where they are coming from. Agreement is not always necessary when understanding is there.

This is helpful for us to remember, because often we skip over that essential part and jump right to the problem-solving. Of course, if we have not really heard what our partner has been trying to say, or how they feel about a situation, finding a viable solution that both partners can appreciate is harder.

Our attitude towards our problems often determines what we choose to do about them. Many years ago, I experimented with this myself. I decided to see if I could change my attitude towards a small problem I was having with something my husband was doing, rather than try to get him to change.

My husband had a habit of going into the kitchen after dinner and having a banana. He is neat and orderly in most aspects of his life, but in this case, he would always leave his banana peel on the counter, even though the garbage can was less than a foot away!

Of course, this seems insignificant, but somehow, when this happened night after night, I began to get more and more annoyed about it. So much so, that after a while, I started to believe he was leaving it there on purpose just annoy me!

Luckily, however, I realized that I might have been making a mountain out of a molehill and gave him the benefit of the doubt. I was also able to recognize that my lovely husband was probably totally unaware that he was doing this.

So, then I was left with a choice—I could either ask him to stop doing it, or I could change my attitude about it. I chose to experiment with the latter. The first night of my experiment, I went into the kitchen and called out to him, "Honey! You left the banana peel on the counter! I love when you do that! It's so cute!"

Now, I do not really know how he responded to this reaction, as he was in the living room at the time. But I continued to do this for several days in a row, and guess what happened? After about a week, I began to feel that this habit was an endearing little quirk of his, rather than a major personality flaw. The experiment was a success and we never had to talk about it.

This was an important lesson in another way as well. I realized how easy it was to let a small situation develop into a

The Problem with Problems

big problem that seemed insurmountable.

Imagine what would happen if instead, we invest our energy into creating a harmonious atmosphere between us, despite the problems. *Remember, whatever we put our energy into, grows.*

There is a popular adage that says, "You can be right, or you can be married." When it comes to marriage, being right is largely overrated and is often irrelevant and divisive.

No matter who is right or wrong, we can always ask ourselves, "What can I do to ease the situation or to make a positive difference here?" This is a more spiritual and effective approach that moves us in the direction of connection and helps us to discover new possibilities.

There will inevitably be some big issues that will surface again and again. Research also tells us that all couples have four or five important issues that they will never agree on. So how do we handle those?

For those unsolvable problems, an attitude shift is essential. Instead of asking ourselves how we can get our partners to agree with us, we can ask, "What are we going to do to protect what's great about our relationship from this seemingly unsolvable problem?" This question puts us on the *same team* and gives a positive spin to a potential problem area.

Remember that it is not what we disagree on, but how we disagree that matters. So, when we do need to come to an agreement or decision, here is a good rule of thumb: Never try to solve a problem until it has been thoroughly discussed, and until you both understand why your partner thinks and feels the way they do.

This is the stage that most of us skip, and then we get stuck arguing about our differences of opinion rather than finding a compromise that works.

Basically, when we encounter something we don't like in our partners, we have two choices: We can get upset about it and try to get our partner to change, or we can make changes in our own attitudes and behaviors.

The second option is the most effective choice if we want to bring harmony into our relationships. Remember, we can never make someone else change, but we reflect on and tweak our own behavior and responses.

So, how can we have a more spiritual and effective approach to problem-solving? Well, we can make more effort to understand why our partner feels the way they do about a problem before we begin to negotiate solutions. We can work on our own attitudes and behaviors first and then team up around finding solutions. When we keep in mind that we are a team and on the same side, we are always stronger, saner, and more successful.

SPIRITUAL PRACTICE

Ask yourself these questions:

1. What are the Irreconcilable differences In your couple?
2. How do you handle your irreconcilable differences?
3. Could you make improvements?
4. As individuals, do you seek to understand your partner's point of view or are you quick to make assumptions, or criticize your partner's feelings?

MARRIAGE MANTRA

I do not agree with your opinion, but I care about you and our relationship, so I will try to understand it, before we attempt any problem-solving.

7

Commitment Counts and Maintenance Matters

Without commitment, you cannot have depth in anything, whether it is a relationship, a business, or a hobby.

—Neil Strauss

Most people get married believing a myth—that marriage is a beautiful box full of all the things they have longed for: companionship, sexual fulfillment, intimacy, friendship.
The truth is that marriage, at the start, is an empty box. You must put something in before you can take anything out.
There is no love in marriage: love is in people, and people put it into marriage.
There is no romance in marriage; people have to infuse it into their marriages.
A couple must learn the art and form the habit of giving, loving, serving, praising- keeping the box full. If you take out more than you put in, the box will be empty.

—From *The Marriage Box*, J. Allan Peterson

Commitment is the bedrock of any successful marriage. For couples to develop deep trust, take emotional risks and plan for their future together, they need confidence in their partner's commitment to them and to the relationship.

It can be really helpful to have a stated commitment in place where both partners express clearly that they are willing to do whatever it takes to make the marriage or relationship work.

We often look at commitment as a one-time thing; we make the commitment once, and that is it. But just like love, commitment is a choice that needs to be restated repeatedly.

By the way, there are actually two types of commitment that contribute to keeping partners strong. The first type is *personal dedication*, which is when we make a promise to work at and develop a relationship that it is mutually beneficial to both of us.

To keep personal dedication high, couples can make sure they are regularly enjoying activities together, making important decisions together, and developing and fostering a shared vision.

One of the most powerful choices they can make together is to take all exit plans or discussions of divorce off the table. This decision keeps both partners feeling safe.

The second type is constraint commitment, where external circumstances secure and re-inforce the feelings of commitment, rather than the partners themselves. This means that even when one or both partners are not wholly committed at any given time in their relationship, other forces can contribute to keeping the relationship going.

Common constraint commitments for couples are things like mutual concern for their children, social pressure from family and friends, finances, and religious or moral beliefs. Other lesser constraints can be things like the fear of dealing with splitting up properties and possessions, the fear of being alone, or concern for a partner's welfare.

The higher the number of constraints a couple has, the

Commitment Counts and Maintenance Matters

more likely it is that they will be able to hang in there through the rough times, when their personal dedication may be low.

Commitment is the foundation that opens the door for couples to become spiritual partners. For our marriages to grow in love, we need to know that someone is committed to us, and the relationship, through thick and thin, no matter what.

Our feelings naturally wax and wane throughout the good times and the bad, but our commitment keeps us afloat in the storm. It is the glue.

Having said that, marriages need more than love and commitment to survive and thrive. They need to be taken care of. Taking care of our relationships is a lot like taking care of our cars. We must fill up the gas tank, so we are not running on empty. We rotate the tires occasionally and check the air pressure. We keep a few things in the trunk to prepare for emergencies. We have an annual inspection to make sure everything is running smoothly.

Our cars need regular maintenance to keep them running smoothly and problem-free, and so do our marriages. We need to prepare for emergencies and reflect regularly on our relationships to make sure problems are dealt with and connections stay strong.

What is the gas that keeps a marriage running? The *gas* in marriage is our *daily loving actions*. We need to be *nice* to each other.

Happy, stable couples show their love for each other on a regular basis with many acts of kindness each day. They feed their marriages daily with compliments, talk, touch, and service.

Most of us know this, but also experience how hard it can be to move from our thoughts to our actions, both in our spiritual lives and in our relationships. We know what we *should* do, but sometimes it is hard to get past our own needs to really do it.

Real love, however, has little to do with how we are *feeling*, and *everything* to do with our personal discipline and capacity for loving. We can always choose to do things within our relationships that will keep us moving in the direction of growth and love.

Life is full of challenges and surprises. But even when we feel tired or discouraged we still need to invest in our relationships to prevent relationship erosion.

When the loving feelings diminish, it is usually because we have stopped investing in our relationships. When we allow ourselves to get lazy with our emotions and our actions, the fabric of our marriage weakens.

Relationships inevitably erode without consistent effort, just like plants will die if we neglect to water them. The good feelings between us will diminish unless we nurture them intentionally.

There is really no way around it—we need to act in loving ways to keep the loving feelings. Maintenance matters.

SPIRITUAL PRACTICE

1. Make a conscious goal to invest in your relationship.
2. Choose to add some benefit or joy to your partner's life today.
3. Make a list together of things you can do to keep your marriage in good working order.

8

Generous Listening

When you listen with empathy to another person, you give that person psychological air.
—Stephen R. Covey

Being heard is so close to being loved that for the average person, they are almost indistinguishable.
—David Augsberger

Listening well, with generosity, is a learned skill. We are not born being great listeners. Since all couples have trouble getting through to each other sometimes, it makes sense for us to evaluate and improve our listening skills.

Listening is usually associated with receiving—but it is a very substantial thing that we can give to our partners. We may have to work at it and practice, but when we do it well, it covers so many other things.

When we listen generously, it is easier for us to focus on building trust, giving value, and expressing our love. And it helps our partners to feel affirmed and really heard by us.

So, let us go over the basics of good listening skills. How do we know when someone is really listening to us? First, they convey it through their body language, their responses, and their eye contact. Of course, it always helps to be in the same room when we are talking, and to turn off our phones.

There are also a few simple techniques we can use to convey our interest in what our partners have to say. The first one is paraphrasing, or repeating back to our partner, what we think we heard them say. You can start with, "So what I hear you saying is...", or "Let me see if I have this right...."

The beauty of this is that when we get it right, our partners will feel heard, and when we do not, they can clarify what they meant so that we can understand it better. Both are positive results.

The second technique is to ask clarifying questions. By asking questions, we demonstrate our desire to understand a person's feelings and intent. We can ask them, for example, "Is that what you mean?" or "Is there more you want to say?"

By the way, there is *always* more! If we do not ask for it, we may not get it. When we do, we allow the person who is speaking to go deeper, and that usually brings us closer.

Another helpful technique is to name the feeling we think our partner is trying to convey. We can say, "It seems to me that you're feeling really angry." Again, if we are right, they feel understood, and if we are not, they will clarify it for us.

When we listen to our partners *carefully*, there is so much we can learn about them. For instance, if we hear them start a sentence with, "Yeah but...", it is a good indication that they are beginning to feel defensive.

This is important information to notice because when we feel defensive, our listening abilities go out the window and we resort to defending ourselves at all costs. Defensive mode blocks any possibility of real connection.

There is one more thing we can all work on and that is to refrain from interrupting—even when we really want to and even when we are sure our words of wisdom will help. No one's wisdom is ever helpful when it comes as an interruption.

Sometimes just being aware of what our goal for listening

Generous Listening

is can make a difference. If we are listening so that we can gather fuel for our opinion, then we will certainly miss the subtle cues and the heart behind what our partner is trying to communicate to us.

The best goal we can have is to *listen for understanding*. This goal adjustment alone has the power to change the emotional climate between us and allows for honesty and vulnerability to emerge.

Really good listening requires effort, practice, and internal strength. And generous listening is a gift we can give our partners to help them feel affirmed, heard, and loved!

SPIRITUAL PRACTICE

Take this quiz and learn about where you might need to improve your listening ability:

1. Would my close friends say that I am a good listener?
2. When people are angry with me, am I able to listen to their side without getting upset?
3. Am I generally able to reflect and validate another person's feelings with empathy?
4. Am I aware of my primary defensive mechanisms that emerge when I am under stress? (such as placating, blaming, problem-solving prematurely, or becoming distracted.)
5. Am I aware of how the family in which I was raised has influenced my present listening style?
6. Do I ask for clarification when I am not clear about what another person is saying, rather than making assumptions?
7. Do I interrupt or listen for openings to get my point across when someone else is speaking?

Now take the quiz again and substitute the words "my partner" for "people" or "person." For example: Would *my partner* say that I am a good listener? Pay attention to any differences in your answers.

Many people discover that it is often harder to be a generous listener with their partners than with others because the stakes are higher.

Take some time to share the results of the quiz with each other and talk about how both of you might improve your generous listening skills.

9

Talking Points

Because even the smallest of words can be the ones to hurt you or save you.
—Natsuki Takaya

You can measure the happiness of a marriage by the number of scars that each partner carries on their tongues, earned from years of biting back angry words."
—Elizabeth Gilbert

Listening well is incredibly important to good communication, but so is the way we *speak*. Sometimes the way we talk can block good communication too, so we need to practice care in this area.

There is an old saying that goes something like this: "Sticks and stones may break my bones, but words will never hurt me." Do any of us believe this adage? Of course not. We all know how powerful words can be. We know they can be used to hurt or to calm, to shock or to love.

Think about a time when you were hurt by someone's words. And now, think about a time when you may have hurt someone with *your* words. Each of us has had the experience of saying something to someone we care about that we later regretted.

Our words have impact. Some individual words have their own emotional impact; think of the words, 'home' or 'family', for example. Don't those two words stir up specific emotions for most of us?

Of course, sometimes it is the way we say the words that matters. Remember when we were kids and our parents made us say we were sorry to our siblings when we really did not want to? Remember the way we used to say, 'sorry', with an insincere tone of voice?

Sometimes it is the emotional association we have to the words that gives them their power—like when a name reminds us of a teacher we loved in grade school.

Since we know that our words have power, it behooves us to be careful how we use them, especially with the people who matter the most to us. Often, we make more effort with those outside of the home—our colleagues or friends, for example—and allow ourselves to get lazy with our partners and children. We mistakenly think that they will understand why we weren't careful, or that they will be more forgiving towards us because they love us. However, even when we understand why the words came out the way they did, it doesn't soften the blow when they land.

Most couples develop patterns of relating that become automatic over time, and we forget to check ourselves and the impact we are having. Recognizing when, and how often, we forget to be careful, is the first step to making changes. To help with this, I often suggest the following to couples I am working with.

Make a goal to stop yourselves from making any negative or critical comments to your partner for one week. Be mindful of what you are saying and the power of your words. I guarantee that if you make a goal like this, you will immediately notice how often you want to be critical, or how often negative things will want to spill forth from your mouth.

And there will be a learning curve here: It is a process of paying attention and practicing restraint. First, you will notice the critical or negative comment just *after* you say it. But do not be discouraged because if you keep at it, you will start to notice it just *as* you are saying it. And then, with practice, you will catch yourself just *before* you say it and you will decide not to! This is the stuff of real growth.

Remember that all growth requires three things: A decision, a commitment, and lots of practice. Being careful with our words and practicing restraint are two important components in the building and maintaining of a strong and healthy partnership.

SPIRITUAL PRACTICE

1. Refrain from making any critical comments to your partner for one week.
2. Make a goal to compliment your spouse every day for one week.
3. Share your experience with each other at the end of the week.

10

A Crash Course in Safety

The ache for home lives in all of us. The safe place where we can go as we are and not be questioned.
—Maya Angelou

Everybody needs a safe place.
—Mary Oliver

A time out is a rip stop; it is the cord you pull to stop a runaway train, a brake, the thing you use to HALT an interaction that either has crossed over into, or is quickly crossing over into, haywire.
—Terry Real

Believe it or not, there is one thing that is more essential to effective communication than generous listening and careful speaking combined.

In my work with couples I have come to realize that the most important ingredient for successful communication is for both partners to feel emotionally safe with each other. In other words, we need to know deep down that we can be vulnerable and honest with our partners, and that when we are, we will be received and accepted.

Conversely, the biggest deterrent to good communication is the lack of emotional safety. When we feel unsafe, we respond defensively, and then all hell breaks loose! The worst parts of our characters emerge, and we yell, nag, argue and attack, or just give up and stop speaking altogether. So learning how to create a safe environment for communication is an essential tool for all couples.

We also need strategies to help manage our personal thoughts and feelings better so that we can connect to our partners with respect and kindness. Successful couples find ways to let each other know when they need to calm down or keep their emotions in check.

I would like to introduce you to a simple technique that you can use to help manage your emotions and protect your relationship.

Having this technique in your toolbox and using it when needed, can be the single, most important thing you do for your marriage. The reason this technique is so effective is because it allows couples to take responsibility together to block unhealthy patterns of relating from invading the good stuff in their relationship.

The first step of the technique is to become aware of the times when either of you begins to lose control or escalate. The second step is learning how to stop your negative interactions so you do not continue to hurt each other. The third step is to return to the discussion when both partners are calmer. The technique is called *Time Out* and here is how it works:

The *Time Out* Technique

1. **Recognize the Signs:** First a couple works at *recognizing the signs* that either or both are getting out of control or becoming hurtful to each other.

2. **Stop the Interaction**: Next, as a couple, commit to saying, 'We need a *Time Out*.' This is harder than it sounds because we are not used to interrupting our fights when we are in the thick of them.

But we need to, because when we get angry or emotional, we change physiologically. Our palms sweat, our muscles tense up, and our demeanor and tone changes because the fight or flight part of our brain gets activated.

This means that we are functioning in survival mode. In other words, "I'm feeling attacked, so I have to protect myself from any threat, including you." The ability to be rational or relational virtually disappears.

Also, a word of caution here: *Never* say, '*You* need a time out', even if this is what you think. It should always be phrased as 'we'. We are in this together and we are *both* taking responsibility to prevent negatives from invading our marriage.

3. **Create a Gesture or Verbal Cue:** Some couples like to come up with a verbal cue or gesture that signals the need for a *Time Out*, for those times when they're in public or in front of their children. Something silly can be helpful to break the tension.

4. **Calm Down:** Once a *Time Out* has been called, then both parties need to do something healthy to calm themselves down.

    People go for walks, pray, meditate, exercise, or watch television. Do whatever it takes to get your body and emotions back to normal. Do not use the time apart to repeat the argument over and over in your heads. This only results in getting more upset.

5. **Schedule a *Time In*:** Before you take a break, agree on a time when you will get back together to resume the conversation. Always schedule a *Time In*, and then keep to it!

> Depending on your schedules and how upset you are, you may only need fifteen minutes to calm down. But if you're having this argument as you're running out the door, or if you are really, really upset, you may need to schedule a time later that evening, or even the next day. No matter what, both partners need to *commit to having a Time In.*

This process of returning to each other in a better state of mind shows maturity and a willingness to work through your hardships.

Taking a *Time Out* is a simple but effective way to signal emotional flooding. With a simple signal, you can communicate to your partner that you are about to lose it, and that if you stay in the conversation you might say or do something you'll regret. And they can do the same.

One more thing to remember: Either one of you can call a *Time Out*, but you agree to honor that request even if you would like to continue fighting. This fosters respect and a feeling of safety between you.

When couples use this technique together, they are reminded that they are each responsible for their own behavior, and that they have the power to stop escalating.

Using it also demonstrates that they care enough about their marriage to stop negativity before it gets out of control and someone gets hurt. They team up and work together to protect their relationship and each other.

SPIRITUAL PRACTICE

1. Spend some time discussing how your couple is doing with regards to emotional safety, noting where there might be room for improvement and growth.

2. Discuss how to implement the *Time Out* technique:
   - Choose a physical or verbal sign or cue to indicate your need for a *Time Out*
   - Agree to respect this as a cue that things are not going well.
   - Brainstorm several ways for each of you to calm down during the *Time Out* and communicate them to each other.
   - Commit to *Time In*.

11

Reducing Toxic Tendencies

"Transformation is much more than using skills, resources and technology. It's all about habits *of mind."*
—Malcolm Gladwell

"You cannot change your future; but, you can change your habits, and surely your habits...will change your future."
—Dr. Abdul Kalam

Every long-lasting relationship or marriage has seasons when the feelings begin to fade. It is a natural part of the ebb and flow of loving. Have you ever heard someone say, "I love you, but I'm not 'in love' with you?" What do people mean when they say that? Do people just 'fall out of love?'

Let us first acknowledge that our feelings are unreliable because they change a hundred times a day. Our feelings can get us into a relationship, but to sustain and deepen a relationship, we need much more than feelings.

When a couple experiences fading feelings, it does not necessarily mean that they have disappeared permanently. It is usually just an indication that they have stopped investing in each other and in the relationship.

When that happens, the good aspects of their relationships begin to get eroded by the bad aspects. If we are not careful, and not paying attention, our selfish and immature tendencies will outweigh our kind and more mature ones.

Research suggests that it takes a 5:1 ratio of positive investments to negative ones to keep a marriage healthy. This means that for every criticism or complaint, we need five positive investments, like compliments or loving gestures, to balance things out and maintain a happy relationship.

It also means that we really need to pay close attention to our emotions, attitudes, words, and actions.

There are a few bad habits that are particularly toxic to relationship success. Recognizing them can help us to take responsibility and change.

The following list is not meant to be overwhelming, or to make anyone feel bad about themselves or their relationship. It is simply offered to help you recognize, reflect and re-start.

Seven toxic tendencies that can erode good feelings

1. *Criticism:* Criticism often shows up in the form of blaming and complaining, or when we begin sentences with, 'You always' and 'You never'.

2. *Defensiveness*: Defensiveness is when we don't take responsibility for our portion of an interaction and defend ourselves instead.

3. *Contempt:* Contempt is criticism that is bolstered by hostility or disgust. It often shows up with eye-rolling, sarcasm, or mocking.

4. *Withdrawal and Avoidance:* *Withdrawal* is when a partner is willing to engage in an important discussion but unwilling to stay with it, and *avoidance* is when one partner shows an unwillingness to get into a discussion at all.

5. ***Escalation:*** Escalation happens when partners begin to respond back and forth in a negative way, and then allow the discussion to get more and more intense. This often happens when we get angry and frustrated.

6. ***Invalidation***: Invalidation is when one partner puts down the thoughts, feelings, or character of the other one. This can be very subtle, like when our partner tells us not to worry about something we are really worried about and we feel dismissed by them. Or it can more obvious, like when we resort to name-calling.

7. ***Assumptions***: This is when someone makes unfair assumptions about what they assume their partner is thinking or meaning. It happens when we hear things more negatively then they were meant, or when we believe the worst instead of the best.

Often the way we feel about ourselves can cause us to misinterpret our partner's intentions. For instance, our partner buys us a membership to a health club so we can accomplish our health goals, but we interpret it to be a disparaging statement about our weight. Or we say something meant to be complimentary and our partner thinks we are making fun of them.

Distractions are another thing to look out for, especially when we are talking about things of importance. Sometimes our internal chatter can keep us from hearing our partners properly.

Other times it can be external noises like the television, or the kids, or the game we're playing on our phone, that can make it difficult for us to concentrate on what our partners are trying to say. It always helps to choose the time and place for serious discussions carefully.

And there is one more thing that gets in the way—and that is our memories. Have you ever had an argument with your partner because you remembered something differently than the way they did?

When this happens, it is impossible for either person to win, unless you have a recording of what really took place. I suggest dropping it altogether.

All of us do some of these things some of the time, and even subtle negative patterns can mean trouble for couples if they continue too long.

So, start noticing which toxic tendencies your couple has, and work together and to reduce and eliminate them. Make it part of your spiritual practice.

SPIRITUAL PRACTICE

Review the list of seven toxic tendencies in this chapter and discuss which ones your couple needs to work on.

12

Talking About Hot Topics Without Burning Up!

You were taught the key to dialogue in kindergarten: 1) Take turns and 2) Don't interrupt. One of you talks while the other listens. Then you switch. This sounds simple. But it's so different from what most people do that it's important to practice.
—Harville Hendrix, Ph.D.
and Helen LaKelly Hunt, Ph.D.

There are two main reasons why couples have trouble communicating well. One is when they disagree about something, like parenting or household chores, and the other is when they talk about sensitive issues like sex or money. It is hard for a conversation to be effective if you are afraid your partner will get upset with you.

When it comes to these more challenging conversations, all couples want to be able to talk to each other with respect and honesty, without being hurtful.

How can we create and maintain a safe and supportive environment to talk about the hard things? How can we ensure that our *Time In* discussions do not lead to more *Time Outs*?

Many marriage education programs and therapists teach

structured ways of speaking for times when couples need to talk about topics that bring out strong emotions.

These methods are similar in that they all have partners taking turns speaking and listening. Using the structures can feel stilted or unnatural at the beginning but gets more comfortable with practice. And sometimes when we do what comes naturally, we really mess up! The structure provides a way to contain our negative emotions and allows for respect to grow.

I call my version *The Safety Net*. Here is how it works:

First, a couple decides who will be the speaker and who will be the listener. Then the speaker will make one or two statements about something important to them.

The speaker speaks in a careful and succinct way. They try to keep their statements brief so that their partners can repeat back to them what they have said and demonstrate their understanding.

The listener will paraphrase or restate what they have heard, checking in with their partner to make sure they have it right. They can even ask, "Did I get that right? Or "Is that what you were saying?" And sometimes they can add, "Is there more?". They cannot rebut or interrupt, even when they want to. It is simply not their turn yet.

Then the speaker can either confirm that the listener understood them correctly or clarify their statement to make it clearer. When the speaker feels their partner really understood what they were trying to convey, they switch roles.

Then the listener becomes the speaker and can respond to what they have heard or simply speak about what is important to them. This technique is not meant for problem-solving. This is what you would use before you attempt to find a resolution. It is a crucial step of listening for understanding.

I recommend that couples practice this technique when

they are not upset so that they can feel comfortable using it when they are. By following the rules of the technique, couples can keep their conversations safe and they do not need to worry about being rejected or hurt.

Using it also prevents emotions from escalating, decreases the chances for misunderstanding, and discourages withdrawal and hurtful comments. When we know our partner will not interrupt or make fun of us, it is easier to be honest. When we know we will have to paraphrase back to our partner what they are saying to us, we are forced to listen attentively and to drown out the chatter in our own heads.

Remember that the speaker and listener have equal responsibility to keep the conversation constructive and positive, even when they are expressing difficult feelings. This means that if one person feels misunderstood, it is their responsibility to do or say something so that the other person clearly knows how they feel.

Using the *Safety Net* technique can get the communication, and the relationship, back on track quickly. Partners will feel more comfortable communicating their feelings, needs and concerns with each other, and can begin to hear the feelings and concerns their partners have without defensiveness getting in the way.

Respect and kindness will emerge in place of contempt when couples team up to create a safe environment to talk about hot topics.

SPIRITUAL PRACTICE

Practice using the *Safety Net* with a few low-key topics that do not push any buttons for either you or your partner. This way you will be comfortable with it when a hot topic issue comes up.

Suggested Topics for Practice:

1. If you received an unexpected gift of money, what would you want to do with it?
2. What is your happiest memory of childhood and why?
3. Talk about someone you admire and explain why.
4. Try talking about a small issue you have and see how you do.

The Safety Net Technique

Rules for the Speaker

1. Speak for yourself—do not assume you know how your partner is thinking or feeling.
2. Keep your statements brief and clear. You want your partner to "get" what you are saying.
3. Stop to let the listener paraphrase and demonstrate that they understood what you were saying.

Rules for the Listener

1. Paraphrase what you hear to demonstrate you really understood what your partner is saying.
2. Focus completely on your partner's message—no interruptions allowed.
3. Remember to ask, "Is there more?" or "Did I get that right?"

Rules for Both

1. Take turns speaking and listening.

13

What Were You Expecting?

When you're dealing with the big issues in life—parenting, intimacy, relationships, goals—your core values come into play. When you're coping with day-to-day issues, such as who's going to make dinner, which car you should buy, how much money you should save, or who's going to initiate sex, it is expectations that surface. Your ideas about how things should be done and what you think should happen affect your choices and your marriage.
—Howard J. Markman, Scott M. Stanley, Susan L. Blumberg, Natalie H. Jenkins, and Carol Whitely, *Twelve Hours to a Great Marriage*

Our expectations develop based on our unique life experiences; the family we grew up in, the relationships we have had, our cultural backgrounds, the influence of media, and other things.

Naturally, we bring all these expectations to our marriages. The problem is that most of them are unconscious. We often do not know we have them until our partners fail to meet them. If we expect something to happen and it does not, or when we have expectations that are unmet, it can lead to feelings of sadness, disappointment, and anger.

What this means for our relationships is that we will be disappointed or happy depending on how well our *perception* of our experiences matches what we expected would happen. This explains how we can be married to a perfectly wonderful person and still experience disappointment.

For example, our partner may have a wonderful disposition and makes us laugh, but if they don't handle the bills the way mom or dad did while we were growing up, we may find ourselves upset with them, and not even really know why. This is the power our expectations can have on our marriages, and why we need to uncover them and deal with them.

I will share an incident here that demonstrates how unspoken expectations played out in my marriage many years ago. When our kids were just getting to the age where we could leave them for a few hours without hiring a babysitter, my husband and I planned a long-overdue date.

We had decided to take a ferry across the Hudson River to an open-air concert on the riverfront. The weather was perfect and I thought that the evening had a lot of potential to be wonderfully romantic. So when I came bouncing down the stairs I was full of excitement for our special night out.

When I got downstairs, I found my husband in the living room completely engrossed in playing video games with one of our sons. I said to my husband, "Hey honey, are you ready to go?" He did not look up but grunted and said, "In a few minutes."

In retrospect, I can see that that was the first expectation that was not met—he was not as excited about this date as I was! And he had not noticed how I looked and then he did not take my hand while we were walking towards the ferry. The date went downhill from there.

By the time we got onto the ferry, I was fuming and completely withdrawn. And my husband was trying valiantly to get me out of my funk, which he is generally quite good at, but I would have none of it.

I wallowed in my disappointment, on the ferry, under the stars, next to my lovely husband, and wasted a perfectly gorgeous evening being angry. He had no idea what had happened or why I was upset, so he could not really repair it. And I could not share it. What a mess!

This experience could have been an excellent opportunity for us to grow and learn about each other in new ways. But at the time, we did not have the skills to dissect it or get out of it. And we had no idea that our unconscious, unmet expectations were responsible.

So how can we prevent our expectations from creating havoc in our relationships? The first step is to become more aware of them, and one easy way to do that is to pay attention to moments when we feel disappointed or angry. These emotions are often a clue that we had an expectation that did not get met.

Once we recognize we have an expectation, the next step is to decide if it is a reasonable one or not. If it is not reasonable—for instance, if we always expect our partner to make dinner even though they get home from work at the same time as we do—then we should just throw that expectation out.

If it is a reasonable expectation, then we need to check whether we have communicated it to our spouse or not. Many of us have a hard time expressing our expectations to our partners.

Sometimes it is because we are secretly hoping they will figure it for themselves or just read our minds. We mistakenly think, "If they really loved me, they'd know what I need right now." But the reality is that even when our partners really love us, they cannot read our minds.

There is another, more powerful reason why we do not communicate our expectations to our partners. We are often just afraid of what our partner's response to us will be. Telling them an expectation we might have requires us to be vulnerable and honest, and that can be downright scary.

This is when we need to decide if the risk of vulnerability is worth it, (and it almost always is), and then find a way to tell our partners what we need and want. Taking emotional risks is necessary if we want to create the marriages of our dreams!

Conversely, when our partners share their reasonable expectations with us, we want to be motivated to meet their needs. That is where the spiritual and emotional work comes in, and this is how we can practice managing our expectations instead of letting them manage us.

SPIRITUAL PRACTICE

Managing Expectations Review:

1. Notice when you feel disappointed or frustrated.
2. Ask yourself what you were expecting that did not happen.
3. Ask yourself if it was a reasonable expectation.
4. If it is not, throw it out. If it is, ask yourself if you have communicated it to your partner. If you have not, take the risk.
5. Meet your partner's reasonable expectations when you can.

Couple Exercise: What are your expectations about?

Explore the kinds of expectations you have about the topics listed below: You might want to write your answers down individually first, and then share them with each other. Make sure to discuss them in safe and respectful ways, and plan for several discussions.

- Power and control: How do you share the decision-making?
- Your sexual relationship—what kinds of things are okay and what is off-limits? How often is good?
- Sexual and emotional fidelity
- Children
- Work and income: Do both of you work outside of the home? Is one job more important than the other? What about when children come along?
- Household tasks—who does what?
- Time together and apart
- Other relationships: Parents and in-laws, friends, and family

14

Fostering Friendship

A friend is someone whose face lights up when they see you.... and who doesn't have any immediate plans for your improvement.
—Bill Coffin

Friendship is one of the biggest expectations that people have for marriage. Most people hope that their spouses will become or remain their best friend. The problem is that over time, we often stop treating our partners in the same way that we do our friends.

Friendships usually make us feel relaxed, comfortable, trusted, and accepted. We do not judge or criticize our friends, and we *do not* try to get them to change. Our expectations are different as well, so we tend to be more forgiving and tolerant of their shortcomings. When it comes to our spouses, however, our expectations are usually much higher because their consequences affect us more.

Friendship in marriage can easily get lost, especially when our conversations tend to focus on needs, problems, and conflict. We can find ourselves spending a lot of our time together figuring out mundane things like who will do the dishes or shop for groceries, and who will take the kids to their swim meets or their doctor's appointments.

To counteract this, it is important to schedule friendship

time that is free from conflict, where you talk without fighting. Think about times when you spend time with friends. Do you argue a lot, for example?

Usually with friends, we might have small disagreements, but we rarely allow them to build or get in the way of our friendships, and we are usually careful not to hurt each other's feelings. We need to behave with our partners in the same way, to preserve the friendship part of our marriage.

It is also important for couples to practice listening to each other the way friends do. How do friends listen to each other? Usually, they listen without blame or anger, show respect for each other's opinions, and demonstrate interest in each other's challenges and experiences.

To create the time for friendship, I think it is important to relegate conversations about problems and household logistics to a specified time. I like to suggest that couples commit to a weekly meeting when they can focus solely on discussing their issues.

Think about it—if you were running a business, it would quickly fall apart if you did not have regular meetings to make sure things were going smoothly. Marriage is no different. It requires constant maintenance and investment.

A weekly meeting can also interrupt the common "nagger vs. avoider" pattern that occurs in most couples. Knowing that they will have a chance to discuss problems every week helps the "nagger" to calm down and stop nagging, and helps the "avoider" come to the table to deal with things in small, weekly discussions rather than putting them off.

Most importantly, if a couple can relegate their discussions about issues to their weekly meetings, they can prevent these same issues from invading and interfering with their friendship time. But a weekly meeting to discuss issues is only half of the equation—scheduling weekly friendship-building time is the other half. Many couples aim for regular date nights to ensure fun and friendship time, but mini-dates can be just as effective!

Sometimes schedules can't handle a full-fledged date, but rather than skip it, substitute a mini-date instead. A cup of coffee in a nice café, a walk in the park, a conversation about what you're grateful for—these can keep the emotional tank full. The main ingredients of regular and mini-dates are undivided attention and some laughter.

Scheduling weekly meetings and weekly friendship time is another smart and practical way for couples to team up and take responsibility for the health of their relationship.

SPIRITUAL PRACTICE

1. As a couple, take some time to discuss the value of meeting once a week to discuss your issues, and choose a time that both of you agree to. Schedule your first meeting and stick to it.

2. Schedule friendship time and treat it as essential to your relationship.

15

Are We Having Fun Yet?

When fun gets deep enough, it can heal the world.
—the Oaqui

Sexiness wears thin after a while and beauty fades, but to be married to a man who makes you laugh every day, ah, now that is a treat.
—Joanne Woodward

Fun is just as important as friendship when it comes to marriage. It is a *necessity*, not a luxury, for marital health and happiness.

Whether couples are in the middle of launching careers, raising children, or in the empty nest stage, having fun together is essential for overall relationship satisfaction and commitment.

However, even though most of us recognize the importance of having fun together, it is still one of the first things couples let slide when they get busy and overwhelmed with life.

There are lots of reasons why having fun together is essential. Here are just a few of them:

- Having fun allows us to build positive memories together.

- Having fun strengthens the friendship aspect of our relationship.

- Having fun provides opportunities for couples to laugh together and enjoy each other's company.

- It is one of the best ways to bond and to re-connect, especially after an argument or a challenge.

Couples will often ask me what they can do when they find that they do not enjoy the same things anymore. This is quite common. Since we go through many stages and phases in a long-term relationship or marriage, sometimes we find ourselves out of sync with each other, and finding things to do that we both enjoy can take a little extra time and energy.

It is natural for people to change, so it makes sense that what we find fun together during one stage of life may no longer be fun during another. Sometimes we have hobbies in common and sometimes we do not. But this dilemma can always be remedied by taking the time to talk about what might be fun for each of you and then taking turns supporting each other's passions and interests.

Even if you do not actually enjoy doing what your partner suggests, they will really appreciate the effort you make to try it out. And you, in turn, will appreciate the same effort when it is offered to you. If nothing else, you will be spending time together, away from the house and the routine, and that can be invigorating—and fun!

Another common challenge in this area is that there tends to be differences between genders in terms of what constitutes fun. In other words, sometimes what a man considers fun is not what a woman does.

For example, when we were younger, my husband would often invite me to go to hardware store with him on a Saturday morning, and I could never understand why. The only thing I was vaguely interested there was the plant department, and that did not take very long.

It took being married quite a while for me to realize that my husband just wanted to spend time together. For him, hanging out at Home Depot together was fun. I, on the other hand, wanted to go out for dinner and a movie. That sounded like fun to me! We realized that we need to compromise a little and started to include both kinds of fun in our schedule.

Remember, these differences are natural and do not have to be stumbling blocks to having fun. When your couple experiences a time when having fun is more difficult than usual, do not despair—and do not give up!

Even if it seems a little strange to have to make effort to have fun, do it anyway. Why? Because taking the time to connect, enjoy each other's company and have fun together are important for the emotional health of your marriage. So, go ahead, and have a little fun together!

SPIRITUAL PRACTICE

1. Commit to scheduling weekly or bi-weekly date nights.

2. Create a "Fun List" together:
   Each partner makes a list of things that they would love to do that would be fun for them. Be creative, do not hold back—maybe divide the list into two: "Things that would be fun for a special occasion", and "Things that would be fun and are inexpensive". They can include things that you have done before and things that you would like to try doing.
   Then, make a schedule and take turns doing something on each other's lists!

Test Your Fun Factor

Take the test separately and then compare notes

- T F I have a fail-safe strategy to make my partner laugh that almost always works.
- T F I am good at knowing the moments when I should avoid using humor.
- T F I can remember something specific we both laughed at yesterday.
- T F We have several inside jokes that other people do not understand.
- T F I would say we laugh together regularly.
- T F I feel safe poking fun at my spouse occasionally.
- T F I really understand my partner's sense of humor.
- T F I sometimes make fun of myself to make my partner laugh.
- T F I use sometimes use humor to diffuse a tense moment between us.
- T F We will often recount funny incidents we have experienced days after they occurred.

Adapted from *The Love List*,
by Drs. Les and Leslie Parrott

16

Marriage is Always an Inside Job

You cannot change anyone, but you can be the reason someone changes.
—Roy T. Bennett

Yesterday I was clever, so I wanted to change the world. Today I am wise, so I am changing myself.
—Rumi

When we approach marriage and relationship as a spiritual practice, it is good to remember that much of the work involved is personal. In other words, marriage is always an inside job.

When we become more self-aware and begin to take responsibility for our reactions and behavior, something significant shifts in our relationships.

Honest self-reflection allows us to step back and look at the interaction between us and our partners with a new perspective. A marriage is a lot like dancing—sometimes we are in step with each other and sometimes we are stepping on each other's toes.

Every couple develops their own patterns of relating to one another, and each person in a couple contributes to the patterns. This perspective gives us new and powerful ways to take responsibility and affect change in our relationships.

When a problem comes up, either partner can change their dance steps and this creates a change in the interaction. Since couples are so connected and affected by each other, any change in our steps will affect the steps of our partners.

The goal here is to recognize this one essential truth: The problems we experience do not lie in our partner but in the dynamic of the relationship or the interaction between us.

If we wait for our partner to change, however, we are essentially, giving away the power in the relationship. This way of thinking also makes it easier for us to blame our partners for things that are not going well, and blame is always poisonous in a relationship.

With this new perspective, we can instead put our energy into *changing the interaction*, rather than the person. It is much more effective, and it puts us in charge.

Since this might be a novel way of looking at your relationship issues, here are four simple strategies to exper-iment with to help you make changes in your relationship dynamic (rather than your spouse).

1. Sometimes Actions Really Do Speak Louder Than Words

Talking can be overrated. It can be helpful but it is not the only effect change. For those of us who rely heavily on verbal communication, this statement might be shocking, so let me share an example from my own marriage to illustrate what I mean.

This was one of the first times that I tried using actions over words, and I was not sure what the outcome would be. My husband and I had been married about 18 years and were in the throes of raising three teenagers. I started noticing that we were no longer greeting each other nicely when we got home from work. We had stopped leaping up from our chairs, putting down the laptop, or coming in from the kitchen to reconnect with a kiss. I missed it.

My first inclination was to sit down and talk about it with my husband. But then I decided to try something different. I decided to see if my actions alone could make a difference, and I made a goal to greet my husband, wholeheartedly, every day for the next week.

Whether I got home first, or he did, I would stop what I was doing, find him, and give him a big kiss or hug. That is all I did, but within a few days, he was doing the same thing.

We never had a conversation about it, I never told him about my disappointment, nor did I ask him to change. I just changed my own actions and created a new and nicer norm in our pattern unilaterally.

2. Change Our Diagnosis

Sometimes the way we are looking at a situation or the way that we are diagnosing it, gets in the way of growth. This happens because the way we perceive and diagnose something, will always inform how we respond to it, and our responses usually make sense in the context of our diagnosis.

For instance, if we assume our partner is being dismissive of us because they are insensitive or mean, our response will be in line with that diagnosis. If, however, we assume their dismissiveness is due to how overwhelmed they are feeling at work, our response will likely be quite different.

When issues come up, it helps to reflect on the diagnosis we are making about the issue, and then ask ourselves if that diagnosis will help us to get the desired results of closeness and connection. When we experiment with altering our diagnosis, we will sometimes find new ways to approach old problems.

3. Beware of Dead-End Assessments

Our diagnosis of a situation can be so powerful that it can prevent our partners and our relationships from growing. This often happens on a very unconscious level—hence the importance of self-reflection. We might conclude something detrimental about their character, like, "He/she is so lazy", which can eventually become a label that they cannot get out from under.

That is when our label becomes a dead-end assessment. A small shift in our thinking, for example, "I wonder why he hasn't taken out the garbage yet?" or "I wonder why she isn't including me in this conversation?" could result in a huge shift in the relationship. What we expect to see is what we will find.

4. Try Something Different

During times of challenge, it is easy to feel discouraged. It often feels to us like we have tried everything, but most of us just keep trying the same things over and over, with perhaps more volume or intensity.

When this happens, it can be helpful to take a step back and ask ourselves these questions:

- What *do* I do when my partner does something that annoys me?
- Is what I am doing *working*? Am I getting the results I want when I do this?

If not, why not try something else? Anything else! We all know that the definition of crazy is doing the same thing over and over and expecting different results. And yet, we do exactly this in our relationships. We continue to nag even though it does not inspire our partners to change, or we withdraw even though it does not help us to feel closer.

Again, if we can look at our relationships as interactions, and remember that we affect each other with every gesture and comment, we can begin to see where and how we can make small changes to build bigger love.

Everything our partner does and says affects us and vice versa. Most couples are so tuned into each other that they can tell how the other is feeling without any verbal exchanges at all. This means that with any little change in behavior, our partners will be affected and therefore, we *can* affect change.

For example, think about what you could do or say to start an argument with your partner. Most of us would know *exactly* what we could do to push our partner's buttons in a negative way.

So, it stands to reason that we could also figure out some small but significant things that might create positive changes. An unexpected back rub, dishes washed, a favorite food, a candle lit. These small gestures can have big impact.

Let us try to remember that most of our problems lie in the interaction between us, not in our partners. This perspective reminds us to pay more attention to what we are doing and saying and helps us to see where we can make positive changes that can affect the way we feel when we are together.

SPIRITUAL PRACTICE

Do Something Else!

This exercise is designed to help you take individual responsibility, and to be more creative with your part in your couple's dynamic.

1. Choose something about your relationship that you would like to see change or improve.
2. Write down the things you currently do or have done to improve the situation (what has *not* worked in the past).
3. Make a list of all the alternative things you could do in response to the problem. Be creative—imagine what you might hear if you were to ask many different people for their ideas.
4. Consider experimenting with one thing on the list, for a trial period of 3—7 days, to change the dynamics of your relationship.
5. See what happens.

17

Staying Open To Forgiveness

In marriage, every day you love, and every day you forgive. It is an ongoing sacrament of love and forgiveness.
—Bill Moyers

The act of forgiveness takes place in our own mind. It really has nothing to do with the other person.
—Louise Hay

It is inevitable that in any marriage that lasts for more than a week, there will be some hurtful times. Many good relationships are destroyed by the resentment created when partners hurt each other. Knowing how to repair emotional rifts and restore intimacy is a necessary skill for all couples to develop.

Successful couples report that being able to forgive is key to maintaining their bond together and one of the greatest expressions of their love and commitment.

For minor hurts between couples, there are three things to keep in mind:

1. Experiment with simple strategies to get the relationship back on track and use the ones that work for your couple. Often, a gesture, a kind word, a cup of coffee

or a joke, is all that is needed to reset and restart the loving feelings.

2. Reconnect as soon as possible. Dragging out the pain and disconnection just adds to the rift between you and erodes trust over time.

3. Stay open to your partner's effort to repair things. When they try to re-connect or repair the hurt, receive it as quickly and as sincerely as you can.

Working to defuse and repair the smaller tensions keeps a couple connected and strong, but there will still be times where deeper forgiveness is needed. Often the biggest hurdle we face is our misunderstanding and confusion around the concept of forgiveness.

What does it mean to forgive someone? Keep in mind that forgiveness is a decision, not a feeling. We decide to cancel a debt, to pardon our partner for hurting us, and to give up the urge to get even or to make them pay. We decide to stop keeping score or reminding our partner of how and when they hurt us.

Let us start by looking at what forgiveness is not. What are some of our misunderstandings around forgiveness? Forgiving someone is not like a magic wand—it does not make everything go away as if the offense never happened. It does not mean that we will necessarily forget the offense, or that we will immediately stop feeling the pain and anger.

Neither does it mean that the person who forgives is denying the offender's responsibility, or that they are releasing the offender from needing to correct the problem. It just means the gates are opened for reconciliation, healing, and the rebuilding of trust.

Staying Open To Forgiveness

Trusting someone means that we have confidence we can depend on another person to do what they say they will do. Trust develops based on our experiences with one another, so when it is interrupted or severed for any reason, it needs to be rebuilt, and that takes time. Trust needs to be earned.

Forgiveness brings benefit to both sides. The person who is doing the forgiving feels better about themselves and can begin to heal. The person who receives the forgiveness is released from their emotional prison and their one-down position.

Being released from the one-down position is a crucial step towards reconciliation. Unconsciously, the person who is in the position to forgive, feels 'better than' the person who needs forgiveness. At the same time, the person who needs forgiveness, feels like they are 'less than'.

It is virtually impossible to have a healthy relationship when one person feels that they are better than the other. The decision to forgive allows for equality and intimacy to resume.

Another misconception we have about forgiveness is that it is a one-time event. Forgiveness is not always a simple, one-time gesture, but more often a process that needs to be repeated several times on deeper levels.

Forgiveness removes the barrier between us so that we can reconnect and move on. And that is ultimately what both partners want! Even though forgiveness can be hard, it is essential to practice in any significant relationship.

Remember, a healthy relationship requires that both people take responsibility for their actions. Both partners need to be willing to ask for forgiveness when necessary, and willing to forgive their partners when needed.

Forgiveness is seldom easy, but it is an essential spiritual practice, and doing it allows us to begin anew.

SPIRITUAL PRACTICE

Take some time to ponder these questions:

1. Are you harboring any bad feelings toward your partner?
2. Is there anything you need to ask forgiveness for? Have you hurt your partner or violated their trust in any way?
3. Are you carrying any grudges over things your partner may have done? If so, how might that be affecting your relationship and what steps can you take to change it?

If the answer to any of these questions is yes, plan to bring it up at your next issues meeting and utilize the Safety Net method to keep things safe.

Even when we understand the nature of forgiveness, it can still be hard to do. It is hard to offer forgiveness and it is hard to receive it. For this reason, it can be helpful to practice forgiveness in a structured way. Here is an example of a structure you can use:

STRUCTURE FOR FORGIVING

1. Make a specific time to work on the issue in question.
2. Explore fully the pain and concerns that are related to this issue for both of you, using the Safety Net technique if necessary.
3. The offender asks for forgiveness.
4. The offended agrees to forgive.
5. Make a positive commitment to change if there any recurring patterns involved.
6. Agree to move forward.

18

Boundaries and Why We Need Them

When you build a fence around your yard, you do not build it to figure out the boundaries of your neighbor's yard so that you can dictate to him how he is to behave. You build it around your own yard so that you can maintain control of what happens to your own property.
—Dr. Henry Cloud and Dr. John Townsend

What are boundaries and why do we need them in relationships? Simply put, boundaries are the limits and rules we set for ourselves in relationships. A person with healthy boundaries can say no when they want to, and not feel like they will be risking the closeness they cherish in their marriage.

Boundaries are about you. When you are clear about your boundaries, you can see where you end, and your partner begins. You can respond to them rather than react, and you are in charge of what you will and will not tolerate. When boundaries are in place, you can maintain self-control and the freedom to choose.

Boundaries are essentially about ownership. In relationships, they help you to have a clear sense of who owns things like feelings, attitudes, and behaviors. And when problems come up, they make it is easier to know who the problem belongs to.

In healthy relationships, partners love and support each other, and take responsibility for themselves at the same time. Boundaries break down when one person tries to take responsibility for or control something that is the other person's responsibility. This often shows up in the guise of helping and gets expressed with nagging and controlling.

Many of us find it hard to recognize the need for boundaries, and to recognize where they can be helpful in our relationships. For this reason, we tend to resist creating and respecting them.

Sometimes we resist them because we feel we are being selfish by having them. Other times we resist them because we want to have control in a way that is not healthy for either person in the couple. The best way to overcome this resistance is to remember that boundaries in marriage are primarily about self-control.

For example, you might want to make a boundary about the way your partner speaks to you when they get angry. However, when you tell them this, they may not be very understanding or supportive.

One reason for this is that your partner's response is not something you can control, and the other is that when you tell them what they can't do, chances are that they will feel you are trying to control them and resist.

Remember that we are setting boundaries on ourselves. We make personal boundaries to maintain freedom and safety. So, how can we make boundaries that are effective and responsible?

It begins by thinking about what you will or won't do, instead of what your partner will or won't do. Instead of telling your partner that they can't speak to you in a certain way, try saying something like, "From now on, when you speak to me in that way, I'm going to leave the room." This is a boundary that you can control. It is about you, rather than them. You maintain control over your personal boundaries, and they have control over their response to it.

Did I mention that this can be challenging to do? It is! It is challenging because boundary-making will always unleash emotions. To make healthy boundaries, we need look within and take personal responsibility for our complex feelings, rather than blaming our partners and harboring resentment. It takes courage and practice, but it is worth it.

Creating healthy boundaries is always a work in progress, but sometimes couples are faced with complicated and serious problems like mental health issues, infidelity, or addictions. These situations may require professional support.

I was coaching a young woman recently and we were discussing the issue of pornography. She told me that her fiancée had recently re-committed to working on his problem with it and had asked her to be his accountability partner. She was encouraged by this, but I was not.

Why not? Well, 'working on it' when it comes to addictions or mental illness is usually just another way of saying 'I'll try.' 'I'll try' often implies that I will make some effort, but I do not have a concrete plan and I may not succeed.

And if I ask you to help me with this, you will end up feeling the burden and responsibility for my failures and then have a hard time creating boundaries around who is actually responsible for the work involved.

This 'I'll try' attitude is just not enough when it comes to addictions and mental health issues, and this is where boundaries become essential. Most people, at least unconsciously, assume they can change and heal their partner if they just love and support them enough.

But if your partner is struggling with a serious mental illness or addiction, you cannot carry them over the finish line. This is something they need to do for themselves. You can love and support them, but they will need to get the professional help necessary to recover from or manage their situation, and oftentimes, so will you.

When a partner is forcing you to live in an unstable emotional reality because of their illness or addiction, by not taking their meds or verbally abusing you when they drink, for example, you will need professional help creating boundaries. Without it, you will be handing over the control of the situation to them, which will be unproductive for both of you.

Whether you are dealing with a crisis or just trying to improve your marriage, the process of developing healthy interdependence is quite possibly the trickiest and most important work a couple will do together.

We build boundaries around us so we can maintain control of what happens to us emotionally. They help us to take personal responsibility and to have control over our own lives, and they allow us to love each other deeply without losing ourselves in the process.

SPIRITUAL PRACTICE

Take some time to ponder and discuss the following questions:

- As a couple, how can we become a stronger *we* without losing the important *me* in our relationship?
- In what ways am I taking ownership of my emotional and spiritual maturity?
- In what ways do we complement each other?
- Are there places where we are trying to control something in the relationship that is not our responsibility?

19

Learn Your Partner's Love Language

If we are to develop an intimate relationship, we need to know each other's desires. If we wish to love each other, we need to know what the other person wants.
—Gary Chapman

Yes, I know there is a whole book about this (thank you, Gary Chapman), but I'm offering a brief refresher because understanding the concept of *Love Languages* can really help us to love our partners better.

We have all been influenced in many ways by how we were raised in our families of origin. We have picked up many unconscious ideas and concepts through our experiences growing up, and one thing that is particularly unique in each family is the way in which they express and experience love.

Our families teach us what love feels like and looks like, and we unconsciously expect to experience the same expression of love, or the same love language, when we marry. Which of course rarely happens.

What does happen is that we speak and love in our own love language, and our partner speaks in theirs, and because of those differences, we sometimes miss the mark.

In other words, we tend to love our partners in the way we

would like to be loved, instead of the way they would. This means that even though we might be loving them with all our heart, they might not always feel our love.

But the good news is that we can learn what our partner's love language is, and that knowledge can help us to meet their emotional needs.

Meeting the emotional needs of our partners is an important aspect of loving well, because it helps them to feel secure. So, if we want to communicate effectively with our partners, it helps to know what their love language is. You and your partner may have looked at these in the past, but it is always good to do it again, partly because we forget, and partly because we change.

A brief overview of the Five Love Languages:

Words of Affirmation: Verbal appreciation, compliments and praise bring instant joy to this type of person.

Quality Time: Giving our full, undivided attention can make this type of person feel special and loved.

Receiving Gifts: This type of person feels the love that comes from the thoughtfulness and effort that is behind the gifts. Gifts have always been visible symbols of love that convey emotional value, and they do not have to be expensive because for this kind of person, it really is the thought that counts.

Acts of Service: This type of person appreciates it when their partner does things to serve them or meet their needs in a practical way. This requires thought, planning, time, effort, energy, and a positive spirit. Anything that we can do that can ease the burden for this type of person, feels like love to them.

Physical Touch: These people yearn for their spouses to reach out and physically touch them. Every kind of physical gesture, like hugs, pats on the back, holding hands, feels like love, concern and caring to this type of person.

So, which love language does your partner speak? What makes you feel loved? Knowing each other's love languages can transform your relationship, because it allows you to love your partners with intention and skill in ways that they can appreciate and feel.

Of course, sometimes it is challenging to love our partners in their favorite language because we are not as comfortable with it. It is always easier to love them in our own. But when an action does not come naturally to us, it can be a greater expression of love.

Here is a personal example of how this knowledge helped in my marriage. My husband and I were married long before Gary Chapman made his significant discovery, but when I read his book, it was obvious to me that physical touch was my love language and not my husband's.

This meant that sometimes I did not feel his love, even though he was very clearly loving me. I needed him to express it more often in the form of physical touch, but I was not quite sure how to bring it up.

One day, after some thought and preparation, I mentioned to him that I really liked it whenever he took my hand while we were walking together. He looked at me quizzically, and acknowledged what I said with a nod, but little else.

It took a lot of guts on my part to bring it up, so I just let it go, but a few days later we were out and about, and he took my hand while we were walking. Well, I was over the moon with joy! It was a double whammy of love! I felt loved because he took my hand, but more than that, I knew he had done it on purpose to make me happy.

This example may seem small, but it is not. It is not a small thing to understand what makes our partners feel loved. When we know our spouse's primary love language and choose to speak it, then their deepest emotional needs can be met, and they can feel secure in our love.

Armed with this knowledge, each partner holds the key to improving the emotional climate of their marriage.

SPIRITUAL PRACTICE

Do you know what your partner's love language is? If you do—congratulations! Now make a goal to communicate your love for them in their love language once a day for a week! See if affects the quality of your relationship and/or helps your partner to feel more loved and appreciated.

If you do not know their love language yet or it has been a while since you looked at this, take the Love Language Questionnaire (www.fivelovelanguages.com) and share the results with each other. Making effort to love your partner better always bears good fruit.

20

When Planets Collide

Gender insight helps us to be more tolerant and forgiving when someone does not respond the way we think he or she should. With new insights, you have the added wisdom and power to adjust your approach rather than seeking your partner to change.
—John Gray

So many of us make the misguided assumption that if our partner really loved us, they would react and behave the way *we* do when we love someone.

But we know that this is not really the case, partly because we are individuals with our own love languages and styles, and partly because men and women really are from different planets!

When we can be sensitive to the unique and different emotional needs of men and women, our understanding of each other increases and can help us resolve much of the conflict in our marriages.

As loving spouses, we want to adjust our interactions in ways that are sensitive to our partner's specific needs, whether they are driven by gender or personality.

Most of us are familiar with some of the more common ways in which men and women differ—that is where all the stereotypes and gender jokes come from. Here is a little review to jog our memories.

Physiologically, we start out the same, but shortly after conception, boys get a wash of hormones that changes them forever. From the moment of birth, girls, on the other hand, are much more responsive than boys when it comes to faces and people.

The sexes also differ in skeletal structure, in that women have shorter heads, broader faces, less protruding chins, shorter legs, and longer trunks. Did you know that the first finger of a woman's hand is usually longer than the third and that the reverse is true for men?

Women have greater constitutional vitality, probably because of their chromosomal patterns. Normally, they outlive men by three or four years in the U.S. Men have a higher incidence of death from almost every disease except three but are 50 percent stronger than women in brute strength.

Women's hearts beat more rapidly than those of men and their lung capacity is about 30 percent less than that of men. And there are literally hundreds of other ways we differ.

Our brains are wired differently, our hormones are different, but most importantly, our emotional needs can sometimes differ.

The way these differences play out in many marriages is that husbands tend to do for their wives what they wish their wives would do for them, and wives do for their husbands what they wish their husbands would do for them.

If, however, we can understand that some of our partner's behavior may be due to the fact that they are a different gender to us, we can develop more tolerance and prevent misunderstandings from erupting into all-out warfare.

For example, men and women often differ in the way they

show love to others. When a woman wants to express her love, she will often try to help that person improve themselves.

But if she tries to do that with her husband, it usually backfires. Her husband will most likely feel like she is trying to fix or change him, which makes him feel incompetent and unappreciated.

Knowing this, when a woman wants to express her love to her husband in a manner that feels good to him, she may need to give him acceptance, appreciation, and respect, instead of trying to improve him. Those are the things that are more likely to help him feel loved.

Conversely, when a husband wants to express his love to his wife, he will often look for a way to help her while she is sharing her heart. So, to help his wife feel better, he may interrupt her to offer solutions, when all she wants is a sympathetic ear.

Men and women also differ in the way that they handle stress. When a man is stressed out or worried, he will often withdraw and retreat until he finds a solution. Women, on the other hand, tend to talk about their feelings to get close and to process their stress.

Another area where men and women differ is in the way they deal with conflict. Men are more likely to withdraw from or avoid arguments and have a lower tolerance for conflict in general. Whereas women are more likely to want to talk about and express their feelings.

In his book, 'Love and Respect', Emerson Eggerichs, offers some insight into another way in which men and women differ with regards to conflict. He says:

"Here is where couples often run into trouble as they try to work out their problems, even small ones. Women confront to connect. The typical response from a man, however, is that he thinks his wife is confronting to control. If another man talked to this man like that, he would sound intentionally provocative. Is that not why some men feel their wives are picking a fight?"

And one of his most significant insights is about women's need for love and men's need for respect. He says, "When a husband feels disrespected, it is especially hard to love his wife. When a wife feels unloved, it is especially hard to respect her husband."

Many years ago, I heard a Japanese/American couple speak about the challenges they faced navigating the cultural differences between them. And at the end, the husband looked at the audience and said, "The cultural divide has been hard for us to deal with, but the differences that came up because one of us was a man and the other a woman, were far greater."

So, there you have it—men and women are different in many ways. With awareness and sensitivity, we can learn to appreciate and navigate the differences with love.

And we have our whole lives to perfect it. Marriage is a journey where we commit to spend our lives discovering the mystery and wonder of each other. And that process, that inner work, is exactly what helps us to grow our spiritual sensitivity and our capacity for loving.

SPIRITUAL PRACTICE

Is there any recurring conflict in your relationship that might be due to gender differences? If so, could you negotiate a way to remedy it?

What's Your Gender IQ?

This exercise about fundamental differences between the genders is just for fun. And always keep in mind that one or both of you may not fit the gender norms anyway!

1. Women are better spellers than men. T F

2. Men are more likely than women to use conversation to solve problems. T F

3. Women have larger connections between their brain's left and right hemispheres. T F

4. Men are better at reading the emotions of others than women are. T F

5. Men score higher on the math section of the SAT than do women. T F

6. In comparison to men, women are better at maintaining a sense of geographical direction. T F

7. Men are better than women at fitting suitcases into a crowded car trunk. T F

8. Women are better than men at describing their feelings. T F

9. Men, more than women, focus their energy on achievement. T F

10. Women, more than men, give priority to relationships. T F

Scoring: Each of these items is based on current gender research studies. Note how many you got correct. The higher your score, the better your basic knowledge of gender differences is.

1-T, 2-T, 3-T, 4-F, 5-T, 6-F, 7-T, 8-T, 9-T, 10-T.

21
Core Beliefs and Spirituality

When a couple shares spiritually, they share ideals, values, and a sense of purpose. They share dedication to some higher good beyond their personal concerns. Such a shared value could be spiritual in the religious sense, but it could also be dedication to art, a political belief, charity, mentoring, or raising children. Relationship empowerment helps us understand that if I win and you lose, we both lose in the long run. In this sense, every form of real intimacy is spiritual.
—Terrence Real

One significant aspect of maturity is the development of core beliefs. Core beliefs are our deeply held beliefs about life, about what is right and wrong, and what really matters to us. Unconsciously or consciously, they guide our behavior and our decision-making.

These beliefs can stem from a religious, spiritual, or cultural framework, but no matter where they come from, our core beliefs can and do have a profound impact on our marriages and important relationships.

When people have strong spiritual perspectives or faith backgrounds, their core values are usually intertwined with their spiritual values. Most people with a spiritual or faith perspective, want it to be a significant part of their connection with their life partners.

Having similar core beliefs generally leads to the enhancement of a relationship. If we share the same faith or the same core values, feelings of respect and connection are fortified, and when couples share common religious and spiritual practices, it often provides another layer of trust and security to the fabric of the marriage.

Shared values also increase our resilience to stress and enhances our personal happiness and health. And when couples connect to faith communities together, they find it offers added emotional and spiritual support for their relationship.

While spiritual closeness is a deeply desired goal for many couples, it is also a common challenge. In fact, many couples struggle to find a shared way to relate to God or to nurture their spirituality together.

This is because even when we have similar faith backgrounds or core beliefs, we usually experience and express them in our own unique ways.

When the differences emerge, we tend to judge each other, because unconsciously we believe that our way of experiencing and expressing our faith is the best way—even while we are trying to make spirituality the center of our relationships!

On the deepest level, we are all interfaith couples, and this reality can create many kinds of challenges, especially if we neglect to honor and respect each other.

Recognizing that there are many paths to spiritual growth can offer us insight into our partner's experiences and choices. For example, some people connect with the Divine while in nature, and some through studying scripture. Others are inspired while in prayer or meditation; still others while caring for people or by participating in spiritual traditions and rituals.

Different spiritual styles work for different types of people, and it is highly likely that our partners will be nourished in different ways than we are. And even if we do not have significant differences now, we can expect that one or both of us will change our beliefs or the way we express them, at some point in our lives.

Here are several ways couples can strengthen their spiritual connection when differences emerge:

- Do not criticize your partner's choices—even if you do not understand them.

- Find ways to honor and appreciate the ways in which your partner experiences the divine and expresses their unique form of spirituality.

- Shift your focus onto what spiritual values you have in common and strengthen that area.

- Find at least one way to express your spiritual values together as a couple.

- Take turns participating in your partner's favorite way of worshipping or expressing their spiritual values. This helps you to gain a better understanding of this part of their lives and help you feel supported.

- Practice being proud of them when they are motivated and growing in their individual spiritual paths.

- Remember that love grows whenever we focus on honoring and respecting each other's choices and internal efforts.

SPIRITUAL PRACTICE

1. Take turns sharing with each other about a time when you felt deeply moved spiritually or emotionally. Your partner's story will give you clues as to how they are nurtured spiritually, and yours will help you to know your own personal style.

2. Share how you could support and honor each other's individual spiritual growth, and experiment with ways to share your growth with each together.

3. Do the *What Really Matters?* exercise following.

What Really Matters Exercise

- Divide a piece of paper into 3 columns. In the first column, list the top 5 priorities in your life. The first thing should be your top priority, and the last the least important. Priorities can include things like your partner, your children, your career, religion, your home, your relatives, and friends—whatever is significant to you.

- In the second column, list what you think your partner thinks are your top 5 priorities.

- In the third column, list what you think are your partner's top 5 priorities.

- Now take some time to look at your three columns and what they mean for your relationship.

- Next, compare your columns with your partners' and consider how your answers might be affecting you as a couple. Talk safely and respectfully and use the Safety Net method if necessary.

From 12 Hours to a Great Marriage,
by Howard J. Markham, Scott M. Stanley, Susan L. Blumberg, Natalie H. Jenkins and Carol Whitely

22

The Marriage Bed

When we touch the place in our lives where sexuality and spirituality come together, we touch our wholeness and the fullness of our power, and at the same time our connection with a power larger than ourselves.
—Judith Plaskow

When we decide to marry, we are choosing to share our lives more deeply with each other than with anyone else. And as we slowly and steadily create trust and safety between us, we are laying the foundation for genuine intimacy.

Intimacy is a tricky thing though because it is not static. Couples move in and out of intimacy based on their behavior toward each other. So, any time we are harsh, critical, or neglectful, we risk weakening our intimacy. That is why we need to identify and acknowledge our part in the demolition process and then discuss what we can do to recapture and strengthen it.

Sexuality plays a huge role in creating and maintaining marital intimacy. The sexual union between husband and wife has always been a symbol of their deep companionship. As couples give themselves to each other sexually, they are forging a deep psychological and spiritual bond.

So how can we become better lovers in our marriages? Greater sexual satisfaction stems from learning how to love better not only in the physical realm, but in the emotional and spiritual realms as well.

Making love is largely about *giving*, and as we seek to affirm our spouses, we are creating an atmosphere of love. Sexual fulfillment has less to do with technique and much more to do with attitude and heart.

Sex has the potential to be a deep encounter of body and soul. In his book, *Sacred Marriage*, Gary Thomas suggests that the true challenge of sex lies in its spiritual mastery. He goes on to say that a growing, healthy, giving sex life is not easy to maintain, but provides the setting for tremendous spiritual growth.

Some of us were introduced to sexuality that had some shame attached to it or have had painful sexual experiences in our past. We bring these experiences with us to the marriage bed, along with our fears, concepts, hopes and expectations. It is difficult to experience the depth of unity and intimacy that is we know is possible, when we are shrouded in guilt and shame.

But our partners, with their love and steadfast commitment, can help us to heal our guilt and fear, so that we can enter a realm of passion and peace, spiritually and physically. And we can offer the same to them.

Sexuality is more than just the meeting of two bodies, it is the meeting of two hearts and two souls. As we mature and develop internally, we bring that growth to the marriage bed, where our love can be enhanced and celebrated.

SPIRITUAL PRACTICE

Talking about sex can be difficult, even in the strongest of couples.

For this reason, some couples find it helpful to create and adhere to a list of things that they both agree on.

It may sound unusual, but by discussing each item, explaining which ones are important to you and why, an environment of safety and commitment can develop between you, which in turn, fosters intimacy.

Model Sexual Contract

1. We commit to being willing and interested sexual partners.
2. We tell each other what we enjoy about each other's lovemaking.
3. We let each other know when we desire sex in clear, positive, and specific terms.
4. We respect each other's sexual comfort and limits.
5. We keep information concerning our sex life private.
6. We let each other know when our sexual needs are not being met within the relationship and make a commitment to resolve the problems.
7. We fill in any gaps in our understanding of each other's sexuality by asking questions.
8. We agree to change our sexual practices to accommodate any changes that occur because of illness, aging or significant life events.

Remember, this is just a model. Feel free to eliminate any statements that you do not like or resonate with, and to add any other statements that are important to your couple. The goal is to list all the conditions both of you need to feel comfortable and safe in your sexual relationship.

This Sensuality Checklist can also help you to get the conversation going:

Read the following statements and decide how well each one describes your current relationship:

0 = never   1 = rarely   2 = some of the time
3 = most of the time   4 = all the time

1. I focus on the physical sensations while we are making love.

    0   1   2   3   4

2. I know what kind of touch pleases my partner.

    0   1   2   3   4

3. I look at my partner while making love.

    0   1   2   3   4

4. I take time to enjoy the afterglow of our lovemaking.

    0   1   2   3   4

5. I use specific sounds or words to arouse my partner.

    0   1   2   3   4

6. I listen attentively when my partner talks to me.

    0   1   2   3   4

7. I make effort to feel emotionally close to my partner while making love.

   0   1   2   3   4

8. I feel confident in my ability to arouse my partner.

   0   1   2   3   4

9. I pay attention to my partner's needs and desires during lovemaking.

   0   1   2   3   4

10. I tell my partner about the lovemaking techniques I like the best.

    0   1   2   3   4

> Adapted from "Hot Monogamy",
> by Dr. Patricia Love and Jo Robinson.

23

Goals, Growth and Guts

To set and work toward any goal is an act of courage.
—Stephen Covey

Attention is the beginning of devotion.
—Mary Oliver

All growth requires concerted effort and clear intention. No one improves in any area without investment. Our characters and spirits are developed and molded through our consistent repetition and practice.

But to be successful, we need to learn how to break our intentions down into measurable and achievable goals.

So, crafting good goals is our first challenge, and is a skill that many of us struggle with. Think about all the New Year's resolutions we have made and broken over the years.

Follow through really matters here, and is extremely hard to do, especially if our goals are either too big or too vague. Most of us have been guilty of making goals like, "This year I'm going to lose weight," or "I will be nicer to my mother-in-law", while neglecting to plan out exactly how we will accomplish it.

I am a huge fan of taking baby steps. When we make unrealistic goals in fits of inspiration, we often find ourselves failing, and then losing power.

A smarter way to make goals is to start small. In other words, we need to make goals that are achievable, so that we can accomplish and experience victory. Little victories boost our confidence and give us the power to keep going and growing.

Weight Watchers and kindergarten teachers have this down—they give stars and stickers for almost everything! And then everyone in the class acknowledges and celebrates each person's small victories.

Making goals as individuals is a skill we all need to develop, but making goals as a couple can be quite different. Therapist and author Michelle Weiner Davis has some helpful suggestions for couples who want to be successful at making goals together.

Her first recommendation is to make sure that our goals are framed in positive ways. In other words, instead of making a goal that focuses on what we want to avoid, we need to craft our goals to focus on what we want to happen.

What we focus on growth and our thoughts have power, so it is never helpful to think too much about what we do not like about our marriage or our partner.

It is much more productive to focus on what we would like to see happen that would demonstrate change and growth to us. For example, instead of saying, "I wish you weren't so sloppy", we could say, "I really appreciate it when you pick up after yourself."

Her second suggestion is that we try to make goals that are action-oriented. Action-oriented goals make it easier for us to experience victory, and for our partners to be successful in their efforts to please us.

To make goals that are specific and action-oriented, it helps if we can describe what we will be doing when we reach our goal. For example, instead of a vague goal such as "I want my husband to communicate better", we could say, "I want him to turn off the TV and look me in the eyes when we talk." See the difference?

One last thing about making goals. What usually happens as soon as we make a goal about anything we want to work on? Opportunities to help us deal with the issue pop up immediately, and challenges that threaten to de-rail us from victory show up too.

If we decide to begin a diet, there will be a party at the office with cake and ice cream. If we decide to be nicer to our sibling they will be on their worst behavior the next time we see each other and push all our buttons.

So, we need to gird ourselves for the challenge, and persevere to accomplish our goals.

Making good goals together is a wonderful way to be intentional in your relationship, whether the goals are financial, centered on your children or about the quality of your communication. It is also another great way to team up around issues that matter to you both.

SPIRITUAL PRACTICE

Spend some time talking together about what you would like to work on, change or improve in your relationship, and then make a goal together to address it.

Make sure to state the goal in a positive way, make it action-oriented, and describe exactly what you and your partner will be doing when your goal is achieved.

24

Editing Your Script

Doing something wrong repeatedly does not make it right.
—Tim Fargo

We have already talked about how each person can make unilateral changes in their interactions, but couples can also work together to re-write old scripts that are not working. Whenever you notice an unhealthy pattern emerging or repeating itself, you can put your heads together and change it.

For example, you might find that you fight about the same issue all the time. Or that your arguments follow a very precise script: "When you complain about the housework, I get defensive and say something unkind, and then you usually start crying." Most of us could just push the "PLAY" button on some of our arguments because we know many of the lines by heart.

These recurring scripts are common to all couples. Remember, we learned how to express love and how to handle our emotions in our families of origin, and we brought those scripts into our marriage relationships.

We absorbed family norms like, "When someone's sad, we ignore them", or "We never talk about finances", or "This is how we handle anger."

Most of the time, these scripts are unconscious, and when

we find ourselves having the same fight over and over, or hitting the same brick wall, it is often because we are operating from our own personal scripts.

This can make it hard to be effective problem-solvers in our marriages. We just do and act the way we always have.

Here is the good news: Every couple can rewrite certain portions of their scripts together. Couples need to be working off the same script at least some of the time. Instead of maintaining frustrating or painful habits of relating, we can decide to create new patterns as a team.

Here is an example of what I mean. I was working with a couple who kept repeating the same destructive pattern over and over, and neither partner felt good about the way they were handling the issue. They had talked about it a lot, and were overly sensitive to each other, but could not figure out how to change the pattern.

One day, in my office, they descended into the pattern yet again and then turned to me and said, "See? This is what always happens!"

This time, at my suggestion, they decided to rewrite the script together. The wife asked the husband to tell her what she could do differently. He suggested something and she agreed to try it.

Then he asked what he could do differently to change his part of the pattern, and she suggested something to him that he agreed to try. They discussed it and tweaked it until they both felt satisfied, and then they wrote it all down.

Writing it down solidifies the new script and makes it easier to refer to and repeat. Once they had created their new script that they crafted together, they started to use it whenever the issue came up. This opened new ways of viewing the problem and new ways of resolving it.

They also planned for times when one or the other might forget the new script and fall back into the old one, and they made a script for how to bring that up to each other without being hurtful. This is intentionality and creativity at its best!

Even though we are creatures of habit, we can still be intentional about co-creating our futures together, and we can start over anytime we want to.

Every couple can do this. It requires effort and honesty and working together as a team. But we can re-write our scripts so that they reflect how we both think and feel in the present moment, as opposed to when we were kids. And what a difference it can make when we do!

SPIRITUAL PRACTICE

Is there an area in your marriage that might need a script re-write? If there is, (and there probably is!), do your best to accomplish a re-write in a way that allows both of you to have input, integrity, and ownership. And make sure to write it down!

25

Tending to Your Spending

Money isn't an easy conversation. We're brought up not to talk about money—and many couples never even talk about where the funds come from for dates and vacations and gifts before the wedding—or even how they'll pay for the wedding itself. We arrive in marriage without much financial literacy. And we come to the subject with two different sets of ingrained ideas, attitudes, and systems for handling money— one for each family of origin. Blending all of that into one system that meets your hopes and dreams and that gets the bills paid is very volatile.
—William Bailey, Ph.D.

Money does not seem to be a very spiritual topic, but managing money as a couple does require emotional and spiritual maturity. Money is one of the most common issues that couples fight about and is an area of stress and conflict for most of us. The problem is that people tend to be emotional and reactive when it comes to finances, rather than strategic and logical.

There are also some differences in the ways that men and women think about saving and spending. For example, people commonly think that women spend more money in a month than men do. Men and women tend to spend around the same amount each month, however, but they spend it on different things.

Women tend to spend their money on household and personal items, whereas men tend to spend their money on large items and electronics. And did you know that when it comes to investing, men tend to be more willing to take financial risks than their wives?

Even though talking about money can be hard, it is important for couples to do it on a regular basis. One reason is because it keeps us accountable to ourselves and each other.

The other reason is that most people tend to lie to themselves about how much they spend, in the same way that we lie about how much we have eaten or had to drink.

When conversations do get challenging, couples need to remember that they may not be arguing about money at all.

Disagreements about money often erupt because of deeper issues under the surface that are not being dealt with. And when that happens, the only way to resolve the financial challenges effectively is to deal with what is going on underneath.

Usually what is underneath is harder to talk about, so we avoid it or don't do it very well. That can lead to guessing and assuming, which in turn leads to misunderstandings, hurt feelings, and resentment.

When we are resentful about something our partner has said or done, we tend to see everything else through the filter of that one incident. This usually means trouble.

Even though it can be challenging, it really helps if we can bring the core issues out into the open and deal with them before we talk about finances.

One way to do that is to write down what we are concerned about and give it to our partners to read. This allows us to gather our thoughts and write them down clearly when we are not upset. And it allows our partners time to respond carefully to what we have written.

When dealing with finances, remember that each of us has our own meaning that we attach to money, and that is often what we are really fighting about.

For instance, one person may have grown up in a situation where basic survival was challenging. Because of the experience of scarcity in childhood, money might come to represent security to them, and that belief might affect their attitudes around financial issues as an adult.

Their partner may have grown up in an affluent family where money was never an issue, and for them, money might come to represent freedom and adventure. Imagine how these two people might trigger and misunderstand each other, simply because the meaning that money has for them is different.

Other things can also impact the way we view and handle financial issues, such as the way our parents dealt with finances, or a previous experience of losing a job or being unemployed.

Our own personalities have a part to play too. We might be adventurous and carefree, or cautious and prone to worrying, and these characteristics also affect how we deal with money.

Our religious beliefs tend to influence us as well, as do the powerful messages we get from both our culture and the media.

When both spouses are willing to explore the meaning that money has for them personally, it fosters compassion, and helps us deal more directly with what is going on under the surface when we talk about money.

What is your partner like when it comes to money? What about you? Keep in mind that it is quite common to be attracted to people who have different ways of handling money than we do.

So, if we experienced financial hardship growing up, we might love to be around people who are big spenders. Until we marry them of course! And then, the very thing we found attractive when we met, can become a point of contention and stress.

Take some time to talk about this with your partner so that you can begin to understand each other's personal financial style. Remember that all financial styles have their strengths and weaknesses.

Financial decisions can be stressful and come with a hefty dose of responsibility. Still, most couples report that they prefer to share the responsibility with their partners and are more satisfied when they tackle decisions together. And making decisions jointly strengthens our trust in each other and our sense of being a team.

If conversations around finances are hard for your couple to navigate, you are in good company. Next time you need to have one of these discussions, take the time to prepare yourselves first so you can approach it with empathy, tolerance, and kindness.

SPIRITUAL PRACTICE

Look at the list below and ask yourselves which of the following things you believe about money. Once you have both done this, share what you learned with each other. Discuss how this understanding of yourselves and each other can help you to strengthen and improve your approach to finances.

1. Money is important: it is hard to be poor and happy.

2. Buying things for people shows how much I love them.
3. Money is dirty and good people avoid dealing with it as much as possible.
4. When I have money, I feel safe and secure; I do not fear for the future.
5. Lack of money is holding me back from becoming what I want to be.
6. I feel better about myself when I have more money.
7. Money means being able to accomplish my goals and feel in control of my life.

26

A Word on the In-laws

Positive in-law relationships are one of life's greatest assets. Living in harmony, encouraging, and supporting each other in our individual pursuits, helps all of us reach our potential.
—Gary Chapman

When we marry, not only do we commit to an individual, but also to building a comfortable relationship with that individual's family members, however quirky or unusual they may be.

It can certainly be challenging when two families collide, but the effort to create harmony is always worth it, because it offers protection and support for our marriages and families.

Getting married always requires flexibility and periods of adjustment, and so does gaining or becoming an in-law. Everyone involved is on a learning curve, so cultivating understanding, and the willingness to forgive is important.

Young couples may find that they need to set some boundaries for themselves, especially in terms of expectations around how often to get together with in-laws.

Here are four helpful strategies to keep in mind when things do get difficult:

1. Your primary loyalty should always be with your spouse. Couples should try to maintain a united

front, stay loyal to each other, and work together to protect the needs of their couple. This is especially important when making boundaries around things like celebrating family holidays, differing religious traditions, parenting styles and privacy.
2. Be careful about criticizing or judging your spouse's relationship with their parents. Your energy is better spent by putting your focus on strengthening and improving your marriage.
3. If your parents criticize your spouse, always stick up for your spouse, no matter what the criticism is about or whether or not you agree with it. You can discuss it later amongst yourselves when and if you want to, but not in response to a criticism from outside the marriage.
4. Use discernment when sharing with your parents and in-laws during times of marital stress. Keep in mind that we do not talk to others about our relationship when things are going well nearly as often as when they are not. Parents and in-laws will always get a skewed version of what is happening and will always find it hard to be neutral.

Becoming an in-law also has it's adjustments, and even if you've been one for a long time, it's always useful to re-evaluate your relationship with your adult children and their partners. Think and discuss with your spouse about the ways in which you are contributing, both emotionally and practically, and on what you could do to improve the quality of these important relationships. Here are some helpful suggestions:

A Word on the In-laws

1. Accept that your role in your child's life shifts when they get married, as it should. Their partner is now the most important person in their life.
2. Do not complain about your daughter or son-in-law to your son or daughter. It puts them in the impossible situation of having to choose between you and their partner.
3. Remember important things about your daughter- or son-in-law's life, their parents and their siblings. Show you care by following up with them on things you talked about in your last conversation.
4. Notice their strengths and complement them. Look for ways to support them and make their lives a little easier.
5. Don't be nosy. They will tell you what they want to.
6. Stay out of their arguments. It's hard to be neutral and they won't be telling you the whole story anyway. Bite your tongue before you give advice—especially if it's not asked for.
7. Be careful to offer advice only when it is asked for. All couples need to create their own unique couple culture, and the space to do so is the best gift parents and in-laws can give.

Negotiating each of these relationships requires extra effort on everyone's part. Whether we are the in-laws or the couple, we all need to be kind and considerate, careful with our words, and treat each other with respect.

SPIRITUAL PRACTICE

If you are a young couple, spend some time talking about your relationship with each of your parents. What could you do to improve them? If needed, how could you team up and clarify boundaries in specific areas?

If you are the in-laws, take some time to reflect on your relationships with your children and their partners. What improvements would you like to see? What could you do to facilitate any changes, and how could you help to create more love and respect between you?

27

Recalibrating After A Life-Changing Event

Knowing that our marriages naturally progress through life stages can help us have perspective. But every marriage will also experience life-changing events that will throw us for a loop. Chances are that your marriage has already weathered one or more of these kinds of events.

Life-changing events include anything that alters your perception of who you are and what your priorities are. They can be good or bad, but they will always be stressful, and require adjustment.

Life altering events can include any of the following:

- Accidents
- Relocating
- Having a baby
- Significant loss
- Blended Families
- Divorce
- Buying or selling a house
- Changing or losing a job
- Starting or changing careers
- Serious illness or death
- Retiring

Events such as these force us to let go of what is familiar and safe, and can stir up feelings of anger, anxiety, and self-doubt. Change on such a scale, make us feel vulnerable and insecure about ourselves, our place in the world, and our future.

You and your partner will likely respond differently to these events, and one of you may be more impacted than the other. Regardless, you will need to find a way through the upheaval, individually and as a couple.

The period after a life-changing event or crisis is an especially important time for a couple. You will need to take stock of how things have changed, particularly in terms of intimacy and connection.

You might find, for example, that the coping strategies that worked during the crisis, are no longer effective as you work toward creating your new reality. If you discover behaviors that are no longer helpful, you will need to re-set your course with your relationship priorities clearly in place.

However, after a crisis, people often notice that their priorities have changed. This means that the way you see the world and the way you approach day to day life can shift as well. These changes will naturally affect your relationship, and it will take time to settle into your new equilibrium.

Big events create big changes, but they can also be great opportunities for couples to reevaluate the direction their lives are taking.

SPIRITUAL PRACTICE

Has your couple experienced one or more life-altering events? If so, talk about they have impacted your relationship. If you recognize some shifts in behavior that you would like to change, brainstorm ways to re-set your course.

Take time to ask yourselves the questions that really matter:

- What do we want our partnership to be like going forward?
- What have we lost that we want to regain in our relationship?
- What are our priorities right now?
- What routines do we need to put in place to help us feel connected and secure?

28

Blended Families

The secret to blending families is... There is no secret. It's scary and awesome and ragged and perfect and always changing. Love and laugh hard; try again tomorrow.

—Mir Kamin

In truth, a family is what you make it. It's made strong not by the number of heads counted at the dinner table, but by the rituals you help create, the memories you share, the commitment of time, caring, and love you show to one another, and by the hopes you have for the future as individuals and as a unit.

—Marge Kennedy

As the divorce rate continues to rise in our culture, so too does the number of blended families, with curremtly more than 3.9 million American children living in households with a stepparent. But just because it's common, doesn't mean it's easy to bring two families together under one roof.

Building a successful blended family also takes considerable time. The American Academy of Child and Adolescent Psychiatry suggests that it can take one to two years for blended families to adjust to all the changes that occur. But when parents work together as a team, and are proactive in dealing with potential problems, they can make the adjustment period smoother for everyone.

Blended families can be messy and complicated and they bring with them unique challenges that are best dealt with before the blending begins. But even if you are already blended, knowing what to expect can give you an edge. Here are some things for you to think about.

As parents you will need to:

- Decide how you will parent all of the children, and what you will do when they misbehave. The discipline rules will need to apply to everyone.
- Come to terms with the fact that your partner's ex is going to be an official part of your family from now on and figure out how to deal with that in the best way you can.
- Realize that one or both of you may have difficulty letting your partner be a parent to your biological children.
- Find ways to have regular communication with each of the children to make sure you know how they are feeling and adjusting.
- Consider implementing family meetings so that every member of the family feels like they have a voice and a place to air their grievances. (Three basic rules for successful meetings are that everyone gets to talk, everyone has to listen with respect, and no one puts anyone down. Oh, and ice cream can help too.)
- Create new traditions for your new family. They don't have to be big, but they do have to be consistent. And make sure to schedule lots of opportunities to have fun and make new memories together.

What to anticipate with your children:

- Your stepchildren may have a hard time accepting you as their parent while they still have another parent. Be patient and continue to invest.
- Stepsiblings will probably have disagreements with each other and will need help from you to navigate them.
- Any stepparent brings new expectations, new norms and old habits, and their very presence often reminds the stepchildren that their biological parents are no longer together. Be sensitive to all the adjustments they will have to make and support them through it.
- The children often feel they are getting less attention, especially at the beginning, as they will have to compete with their new siblings and their parent's new partner. Parents can compensate by making sure each child gets undivided attention on a regular basis.

Becoming a part of a blended family will naturally have it's ups and downs. Both the adults and the children will sometimes make mistakes and hurt each other's feelings, but everyone needs to adjust to the new situation in their own way and in their own time. Keep in mind that closeness is built over repeated interactions, and develops at its own pace.

Since parenting in a blended family can bring up many issues for couples, it's important that you take of yourselves, keep your discussions safe, and get help if you need it. Never forget that your unity is the backbone for your new family.

It takes hard work and patience to create a happy, healthy blended family, but the bonds you will build are worth the effort and will last a lifetime.

BLENDED FAMILY MANTRA

The best recipe for a happy blended family is:

3 cups love
1 cup empathy
1/4 cup patience
and 1 tablespoon teamwork

29

Seasons of Love

A successful marriage requires falling in love many times, always with the same person.
—Mignon McLaughlin

It is natural that relationships grow and change over time. In marriage, however, it is helpful to know that there are specific, defined stages that all couples go through, and that each of these stages provide us with new challenges and require us to learn new skills.

Knowing that these stages are normal can give us perspective when we find ourselves in the middle of one, especially if we are really struggling. Here is a brief explanation of each stage to help you recognize and reflect on where your couple might be.

Keep in mind that you may be somewhere in-between two stages, and that we often vacillate between them as we tackle the skills we need to learn.

Stage One: Passion and Promise

This stage is often referred to as the "honeymoon" stage and can last anywhere from two months to two years. You have fallen in love and know that this is the person you want to spend the rest of our life with. It is full of effortless communication, sharing dreams and romance, and it feels as though everything is possible.

Stage Two: Disillusionment

This is when the honeymoon stage begins to fade and reality sets in. You begin to see your partner for who they really are, with all their habits and flaws.

As the differences between you become more apparent, you may start to argue more and find yourselves feeling like opponents rather than a team.

This stage usually coincides with a time when you will be making big decisions about careers, finances, and children, which can increase the stakes of your discussions and problem-solving efforts.

Your main job at this stage is to learn how to communicate better and resolve conflict more effectively.

Stage Three: Misery

Many couples struggle to develop new skills around communicating, negotiating and problem-solving. But when couples discover that they cannot resolve issues in a mutually agreeable way, resentment and mistrust invades.

We cannot always live up to each other's expectations, and we will, unintentionally, disappoint and hurt each other. As we become more aware of our differences, we can find ourselves enmeshed in power struggles and narrow thinking about who is right and who is wrong.

A necessary task during this stage is to figure out how to honor both our own, and our partner's, individuality and independence, while still maintaining closeness as a couple.

Anxiety and fear can easily enter a relationship at this point as we feel the balance is being threatened, and this can bring out our worst behavior. We can easily find ourselves slipping into blame, criticism, and defensiveness in order to cope with change.

During this stage, you will also need to learn how to deal with anger and hurt in healthier ways. You will need to practice forgiveness on a regular basis, and you may need to get new types of help and support.

A couple in this stage is faced with three choices:

1. They give up. They feel like they have tried everything, or that they married the wrong person and they start thinking about divorce.
2. They decide to settle for less. Discouragement sets in and some couples to decide to lead separate lives.
3. They decide to learn healthier and more productive ways of interacting.

The pain can be so intense during this stage, that it can feel overwhelming. A couple in this stage is trying to re-create a new and better version of themselves, and it can feel impossible at times.

But if they persevere, and learn the necessary skills, they can break through to the next stage, and experience security and joy.

Stage Four: Awakening and Acceptance

This is the stage where the pain and hard work of the earlier stages really begins to pay off. You begin to approach life as a team and develop a sense of pride for what you have overcome together. You can appreciate your partner's sense of commitment to making your marriage last and you feel a greater, overall acceptance for them and the relationship.

In this stage, you finally stop trying to get your partner to change and begin to accept them for who they really are, and it is easier to resolve disagreements and to forgive each other. Friendship, commitment, and trust deepen and both partners feel more confident in the relationship.

You understand each other's strengths and vulnerabilities and learn to identify and talk about your fears. As you stop criticizing and blaming, empathy and compassion for each other increases. You learn to appreciate and respect each other in new ways, and develop a new balance of separateness and togetherness, interdependence, and intimacy.

This kind of marriage is what we are all after. And it is very possible! The trouble is that we forget that these stages are natural and essential to our growth as couples, and that they require us to learn new skills.

So, let us remember that a stage is just a stage and not a destination. Each challenge and each victory brings us closer to developing a deeper intimacy and mutual respect.

As Robert Browning so beautifully wrote: "Grow old with me—the best is yet to be."

SPIRITUAL PRACTICE

Discussion Points:

1. What season is your marriage in right now? Are you in-between seasons?
2. What tasks are you being challenged to accomplish?
3. Is there any area where one or both of you feel stuck? If so, help each other to make small, practical goals that can enable you get "unstuck".

29

Becoming a Blessing to Each Other

We need a witness to our lives. There is a billion people on the planet... I mean, what does anyone life really mean? But in a marriage, you're promising to care about everything. The good things, the bad things, the terrible things, the mundane things... all of it, all the time, every day. You're saying, 'Your life will not go unnoticed because I will notice it. Your life will not go unwitnessed because I will be your witness.
—Shall We Dance?

As spiritual partners, we are responsible for our own internal growth, and that of our couple. In both instances we are consciously developing healthier habits and patterns that help us to be more present.

When things are going well, our loving interactions with each other can provide us with the inspiration and motivation to reach out and help others and when we bring the energy of service back into our marriage, it is strengthened.

When two individuals are contributing and giving outside of their marriage, they naturally receive power from that giving, and it spills over into the marriage relationship. And when the marriage is growing and healthy, that gives each spouse more power to give outside of the family. It is a perfect plan.

And as we become more intentional in our choices, and work towards building and maintaining authentic connections with each other, we naturally become co-creators of our marriage.

As we realize that love is a daily decision that we make, not just a feeling we have towards someone, we can back up our choices with conscious actions. We can shift out of automatic pilot and move into awareness and intention.

As we do so, we are blessing each other with our support, our love, and our attention. We become blessings to each other as we give our partners the support and the confidence to become their best selves.

SPIRITUAL PRACTICE

We have the ability, opportunity, and privilege to speak or give a blessing to our partners every day, in a way that communicates honor, value and encouragement.

1. Ask yourself how you could be a blessing to your partner today.
2. What could you say to encourage, honor and remind them of their intrinsic value?
3. How can you demonstrate that you are a witness to their lives? That you see them in the deepest way?

30

Small Steps to Bigger Love

The truest form of love is how you behave toward someone, not how you feel about them.
—Steve Hall

The real act of marriage takes place in the heart, not in the ballroom or church or synagogue. It is a choice you make—not just on your wedding day, but repeatedly—and that choice is reflected in the way you treat your husband or wife.
—Barbara de Angelis

I think it helps when couples can agree on some basic rules of conduct. Just like when we are playing a game or a sport, we need agreed upon rules before we can enjoy the game. It is the same with marriage. Marital rules of conduct can help to minimize conflict and provide guidelines for couples when dealing with difficult matters.

There are many things that contribute to the development of a happy relationship that continues to grow and thrive. Here are some of my favorites:

Small Steps to Bigger Love

1. Never threaten divorce no matter how upset you get.
2. Use the *Time Out* technique to prevent emotional erosion.
3. Have regular meetings to discuss issues and problems.
4. Aim for a 5:1 ratio of positive to negative interactions every day.
5. Make time for friendship, fun, and laughter.
6. Remember that marriage requires a profound respect for differences.
7. Develop a positive bias towards your partner—look for the gold.
8. The first five minutes together after being apart really matter, so make them count.
9. Use the *Safety Net* technique to keep things safe.
10. Ask yourselves, "Is what I'm about to say going to bring me closer to my goal of connection or not?"
11. Take a few minutes every day to be completely present to the person you share your life with.
12. Ask, "What can I do to improve this situation? How can I take responsibility for my part in our dynamic?"
13. What you want to *last* should come *first*—so give your *best* to the person you say you love the most, instead of the leftovers. It is not OK to be nice to everyone else all day long and then dump on your partner when you get home.
14. The vision we have for our marriage largely determines the outcome, so work on your vision together and make it crystal clear.

15. Bless your partner with encouragement and attention every day.

Simply Speaking

When we look at our relationships as central to our spiritual and emotional growth, we are forced to pay attention to our actions and attitudes. Obstacles become opportunities for growth, and our marriages and families become the places where our most significant growth occurs.

ONGOING SPIRITUAL PRACTICE

Spiritual practice in marriage all boils down to doing these two things:

1. When I get upset with my partner, I will ask myself this question: If I want to be true to my core beliefs, how should I respond in this moment?
2. I will strive to relate to the *person* I married, not their *behavior*. I will look for the gold in my partner.

Small Group Study Guide

Studying this book with a small group of couples can be a wonderful experience. When couples study about marriage and relationship together, they discover very quickly that other people struggle with the same things they do. It is both healing and empowering to be able to laugh at and discuss these challenges together.

The study guide provides discussion questions to enrich the group experience. The following is a suggestion for how to study the book in a group situation and can be adapted to meet the unique needs of any group.

I recommend that before you begin meeting as a group, you take time to agree on basic guidelines like the ones suggested below. This will ensure the best experience and outcome possible for everyone.

Guidelines for a Successful Small Group

1. Confidentiality: We will maintain complete confidentiality. What we hear and say, stays within the group.

2. Mutual Respect/No Put-Downs: Critique ideas, but not people.

3. No Interruptions: Let people finish talking.

4. Use a Timer to facilitate equal time for sharing.

5. Accountability: We will show up for every session unless we are out of town or we have let the host know the (good) reason we will be absent.

6. Affirmation: We acknowledge that every person (couple) is at a different point in their marriage, and we will value and affirm people for who they are and where they are at.

7. Listening: We understand that others might need to be encouraged to share, to be open and to show emotion. We will let them do so, without being judgmental, trying to fix them, or offering unsolicited advice.

8. Self-Awareness: We understand that some of us are talkers and some of us are quieter, so we will be aware of not dominating the discussion or always leaving the weight of it to others.

9. Vulnerability: We will stretch ourselves to be as open and honest as we can to create a safe environment that encourages others to be vulnerable as well.

—Adapted from Crosswords

Small Group Study Guide

Directions for conducting small group study:

To facilitate discussions in a group situation, several chapters have been grouped together for each session. A few have been omitted because the discussions work better among couples, rather than in a group discussion..

Couples will be responsible to read specific chapters and do the spiritual practices suggested after each one, before attending each session.

SESSION 1

Before Session 1 read:

Chapter 1:   Marriage as a Spiritual Practice
Chapter 2:   Whole Mates or Soulmates?
Chapter 3:   Oh The Questions We Ask!

Do each spiritual practice and suggested exercise before the session.

Discussion Questions

1. Share with the group the ways in which your partner has helped you to grow.

2. Which of the five questions at the end of "Oh the Questions We Ask!" would you say had the biggest impact on you?

3. Do you see your marriage as part of your spiritual practice or separate from it? Does your perspective help you or hinder you in your spiritual and emotional development?

SESSION 2

Before Session 2 read:

Chapter 4: How to Change Your Partner
Chapter 5: Notice and Appreciate the Good Things
Chapter 6: The Problem with Problems

Do each spiritual practice and suggested exercise before the session.

Discussion Questions

1. Share what you learned from doing the spiritual practices with your partner.

2. What are some of the recurring problems your couple has faced and when have you been successful dealing with them?

3. Share one of your irreconcilable differences and how it has affected your couple. Talk about ways to improve negotiations going forward.

4. Have each person share something they appreciate in their partner.

SESSION 3

Before Session 3 read:

Chapter 7:   Commitment Counts & Maintenance Matters

Do each spiritual practice and suggested exercise before the session.

Discussion Questions

1. Discuss the difference between personal dedication and constraint commitment.

2. What kind of commitment did you observe in your parents' relationship? How did your parents' relationship affect your beliefs about commitment?

3. What does commitment mean to you? How is it expressed in your marriage?

4. Discuss the importance of maintenance and investment in marriage. What have you done in the past as couples to invest in your relationship on a regular basis?

SESSION 4

Before Session 4 read:

Chapter 8:   Generous Listening
Chapter 9:   Talking Points
Chapter 10: A Crash Course in Safety

Do each spiritual practice and suggested exercise before the session.

Discussion Questions

1. Share what you learned about yourself after taking the two versions of the *Listening Quiz* at the end of the Generous Listening chapter.

2. If you made a goal as a couple to refrain from any critical comments for a week, how did it go? If you didn't, why not?

3. If you feel comfortable doing so, share about the last time you really felt listened to by your partner. What were the circumstances and what did your partner do to make you feel heard? How did it feel to be listened to?

4. What do you think about the *Time Out* technique? Was there resistance to trying it? Do you think it might be helpful to use? Have any of you tried it yet? If so, what happened?

SESSION 5

Before Session 5 read:

Chapter 11: Reducing Toxic Tendencies
Chapter 12: Talking About Hot Topics Without Burning Up

Do each spiritual practice and suggested exercise before the session.

Discussion Questions

1. Discuss the importance of respect in marriage.

2. Which of the toxic tendencies do you want to work on and why?

3. Discuss how using the *Safety Net Technique* could be helpful. Discuss what misgivings or uncomfortable feelings you might have about trying it.

4. Using stress-free topics, practice with your partner and then with other members of your small group.

SESSION 6

Before Session 6 read:

Chapter 13: What Were You Expecting?
Chapter 14: When Planets Collide

Do each spiritual practice and suggested exercise before the session.

Discussion Questions:

1. Share what you learned as couples when you did the exercise on expectations.

2. Share a time when you felt disappointed about something in the relationship and were uncomfortable talking to your partner about it.

3. Talk about what concepts or expectations you may have had about gender roles before you got married.

4. Discuss how gender roles have come up in your relationships since and how they may have changed.

SESSION 7

Before Session 7 read:

Chapter 15: Fostering Friendship
Chapter 16: Are We Having Fun Yet?

Do each spiritual practice and suggested exercise before the session.

Discussion Questions:

1. Discuss the value of meeting once a week to talk about issues. Which issues might come up for your couple?

2. Discuss the value of date nights and mini-dates, and why they can be hard to implement on a regular basis.

3. Share about the last date you had and/or what activities your couple came up with when you made your fun list.

SESSION 8

Before Session 8 read:

Chapter 17: Marriage is an Inside Job
Chapter 18: Staying Open to Forgiveness

Do each spiritual practice and suggested exercise before the session.

Discussion Questions:

1. Share about a time when blaming your partner blocked growth and intimacy and what you did about it.

2. Is there a situation going on currently in your relationship where you might make some progress if you changed your diagnosis?

3. Discuss what you learned about yourself when you did the *Repair Attempts Questionnaire*.

4. What do you think about the concept that forgiveness is a decision?

Small Group Study Guide

SESSION 9

Before Session 9 read:

Chapter 18: Boundaries and Why We Need Them

Do each spiritual practice and suggested exercise before the session.

Discussion Questions:

1. What was your main takeaway from this chapter?
2. What kind of good boundaries do you have in your relationship?
3. What gets in the way of healthy boundaries in your relationship?
4. Share about a time when you realized you needed to make boundaries in a relationship other than your marriage. How did you do that?

SESSION 10

Before Session 10 read:

Chapter 21: Core Beliefs and Spirituality

Do each spiritual practice and suggested exercise before the session.

Discussion Questions:

1. What did you learn from doing the *What Really Matters* exercise.

2. Discuss the difference between spirituality and religion and the importance of both or either of them in your relationships.

3. Talk about how you deal with, or have dealt with, any differences between you and your partner with regards to spirituality or core beliefs.

4. Discuss the value of equality in marriage, and share about a time when the balance was off in your relationship.

5. Share ways in which your couple has strived to create common spiritual or core-value practices.

SESSION 11

Before Session 11 read:

Chapter 25: Tending to Your Spending
Chapter 26: A Word on the In-Laws

Do each spiritual practice and suggested exercise before the session.

Discussion Questions:

1. Share what you learned about the meaning that money holds for you and your partner.

2. Talk about any goals you have to improve your approach to finances as a couple.

3. If you are an older couple with married children, share any challenges you may be having with them or their spouses. Talk about any new ideas you may have based on the reading.

4. If you are a young couple, share any challenges you may be having with your parents and in-laws. Talk about any new ideas you may have based on the reading.

5. How healthy are your boundaries in terms of your in-law relationships? How would they answer this question about you?

SESSION 12

Before Session 12 read:

Chapter 27: Recalibrating After a Life-Changing Event
Chapter 28: Seasons of Love

Do each spiritual practice and suggested exercise before the session.

Discussion Questions:

1. What season of love is your marriage currently in? What lessons are you learning? Where are you stalled?

2. Share about a life-altering event you and your partner experienced and describe how it affected your marriage.

3. Discuss how you recuperated as a couple.

SESSION 13

Before Session 13 read:

Chapter 29: Becoming a Blessing to Each Other
Chapter 30: Small Steps to Bigger Love

Do each spiritual practice and suggested exercise before the session.

Discussion Questions:

1. What do you think of the concept of becoming a blessing to your partner?

2. Share about a time when you felt your partner was a blessing to you.

3. Do you think it's a good idea to have some agreed upon marital rules of conduct?

4. Which of the ones listed seem most important to you and your relationship?

About the Author

Debby has a Bachelor of Science in Community and Social Change and studied at the Blanton Peale Institute for Pastoral Counseling in NYC. She has trained in multiple marriage and relationship education programs, including Divorce-Busting (Michelle Weiner Davis), the Gottman Method, and the Prevention and Relationship Enhancement Program (PREP).

She has authored curricula on relationship skills for adolescents and young adults, marriage preparation, marriage enrichment, media literacy and pornography addiction. She has taught workshops and seminars internationally and helped countless individuals and couples through her coaching practice.

Whether she is writing, teaching or coaching, she offers a unique, comprehensive approach that is both respectful and compassionate. Her goal is to provide tools and strategies that people can implement immediately, so they can grow in their confidence and their capacity to live and love successfully.

For information on couple coaching or to book Debby for an event or seminar, contact her at coachgullery@gmail.com.